I0124049

Edward Thomas

Early Sassanian Inscriptions, Seals and Coins

Edward Thomas

Early Sassanian Inscriptions, Seals and Coins

ISBN/EAN: 9783741163418

Manufactured in Europe, USA, Canada, Australia, Japa

Cover: Foto ©Thomas Meinert / pixelio.de

Manufactured and distributed by brebook publishing software (www.brebook.com)

Edward Thomas

Early Sassanian Inscriptions, Seals and Coins

EARLY SASSANIAN INSCRIPTIONS,

SEALS AND COINS.

BY

EDWARD THOMAS, Esq.,

LATE OF THE EAST INDIA COMPANY'S BENGAL CIVIL SERVICE.

LONDON:

TRÜBNER & Co., 60, PATERNOSTER ROW.

1868.

STEPHEN AUSTIN,

PRINTER, HERTFORD.

PREFACE.

The original design of the present Memoir was limited to the introductory classification of the Pehlvi Inscriptions of the early Sassanidæ, and the embodiment of their texts in a printed form, as a preliminary measure towards an ultimate correction and amplification, *in situ*, which the seeming promise of the available materials might perchance secure for them from enterprising philologers or antiquarians.

At the commencement, the leading interest seemed to centre in the long though broken Inscription at Páï Kúlí, and it was chiefly the desire of placing a transcript of these epigraphs before the public, in their cognate Pehlvi type, that suggested the article which appears in the Journal of the Royal Asiatic Society.

As, however, the enquiry proceeded, a far more extended series of inscriptions, of similar character, were found to exist, though chiefly accessible only in the unsatisfactory form of artists' copies; these were also subjected to the process of definition in type, and are ready for direct revision from the sculptured originals. Up to this point my intention had been merely to act as the clerical preparer of the imperfect materials which were to serve as a basis for more exact data and more crucial tests, to be contributed by others; but as my attention was excited by the singular phraseology and the subject matter to be found in the Hájíábád manifesto of Sapor, I ventured upon a tentative analysis of that document, and completed the preliminary study of the subject by a full examination and synopsis of the alphabets in which these inscriptions were written, and likewise supplemented to the body of the essay illustrations derived from coins and gems, concluding with an attempt to trace the initial date and eastward spread of the associate Pehlvi alphabets during the Parthian domination.

CONTENTS.

SASSANIAN INSCRIPTIONS.

So long ago as the year 1847, during a temporary absence from my duties in India, I volunteered to undertake the classification of certain imperfectly determined and but partially deciphered series of coins in the East India House collection—in continuation and completion of Professor Wilson's comprehensive description of the more popular departments of Central-Asian Numismatics already embodied in his Ariana Antiqua. Among the subdivisions so treated may be cited the Kufic Mintages of the Ghaznavides, a detailed notice of which was inserted in the Journal of the Royal Asiatic Society in 1848 (vol. ix.),[1] as well as a second article, bearing more immediately upon the subject under review, on "the Pehlvi Coins of the early Muhammadan Arabs," which appeared in the twelfth volume of that Journal. In entering upon the examination of the available specimens of the latter class of national representative currencies, I found myself called upon to encounter a novel and very difficult branch of Oriental Palæography, the study of which, indeed, had but recently been inaugurated by the publication of Professor Olshausen's most instructive work "Die Pehlwie-Legenden:"[2] while it was manifest that the obscure language, of which this imperfect alphabet constituted the graphic exponent, was dependent for its elucidation upon still more fragmentary and defective grammatical or lexicographical means: obstacles which the since accelerated progress of modern ethnography has, up to this time, failed to remove. Under these conditions I

[1] A further paper on the same subject will be found in vol. xvii. J.R.A.S. for 1858.

[2] Die Pehlwie-Legenden auf den Münzen der letzten Sâsâniden, etc. Kopenhagen, 1843. A translation of this work is to be found in the London Numismatic Chronicle, vol. ix., 1846.

naturally approached this new investigation with sufficient diffidence, and sought to secure the critical soundness of any suggestive deductions that might present themselves, by a decisive appeal to every archæological test within reach. Foremost among these were the monumental writings of the earlier Sassanian kings, who, in traditional imitation of the Achæmenians, from whom, indeed, they boasted a but temporarily obscured descent—indulged ostentatiously in mural sculpture and attendant lapidary epigraphy. The Rock Inscriptions of Ardashír Bábekán and his proximate successor are couched in duplicate versions, varying dialectically, and written in mere modifications of the same normal alphabet; the one ordinarily employed to define the Pehlvi of Eastern Persia, and out of whose literal elements modern Zend was elaborated, is now conventionally termed "Sassanian:" its counterpart transcript, which adheres more closely to Chaldæan literal forms, was once designated "Parthian," from its occasional official employment under that intrusive dynasty, but has latterly been known as Chaldæo-Pehlvi. The parallel versions of the original inscription of Sapor I. in the Hájíábád Cavern, which had been secured many years ago in the form of direct plaster impressions by Sir E. Stannus,[1] sufficed to furnish a thoroughly trustworthy outline of the manipulative type of each letter of the concurrent alphabets; these forms were separately compared, selected examples copied, and, finally, the duplicate series were incorporated into a classified table, which may be cited with still undiminished confidence, as freely representing the epochal current forms of the joint Pehlvi characters, and as furnishing an efficient illustration of the divarications from a given standard gradually introduced in succeeding ages.

On a later occasion, following up the same subject, I availed myself of another hopeful source of palæographic data, afforded by the signets and seals of the Persian nation at large, fabricated during the period of the Sassanian rule,

[1] The original impressions are now in Dublin; secondary casts are to be found in the Assyrian Room in the British Museum, and the Royal Asiatic Society possesses parallel reproductions. It is from the latter that the illustrative Photograph has been derived.

the identificatory legends of which almost uniformly followed the Eastern type of the concurrent systems of writing. I had scarcely, however, arranged my materials for the elucidation of this branch of the enquiry, when I was called upon to return to the scene of more important avocations; but desiring that the various Antiquarian remains I had succeeded in bringing together should be placed at the disposal of those who might, perchance, have both greater leisure and ability to do justice to the study, I published a cursory notice, pretending to be little more than an introductory explanation of the contents of the three plates of gem and other legends already prepared, which figure in the thirteenth volume of the Journal of the Royal Asiatic Society.

The leading object of the present notice, as confessedly preliminary and tentative as its predecessors, is to draw the attention of resident European officials or chance travellers in the East to an elaborate biliteral inscription, originally engraved along the face of the terrace of the Fire Temple at Páï Kúlí[1] (lat. 35° 7′ 16″ N., long. 45° 34′ 35″ E.), eye transcripts of which were made, under considerable disadvantages, by Sir H. Rawlinson and Mr. Hector in 1844, and from whose pencil *facsimiles* the modernized version now printed has been derived.

Sir Henry Rawlinson describes the present condition of the engraved slabs as anything but promising for the acquisition of a full and complete copy of the ancient writings. The inscribed stones, which formed the terrace-wall supporting the edifice, are stated to have become displaced, and to have mostly rolled down the slope of the hill at hazard, so that their relative continuity would with difficulty be re-established, even if in the majority of cases the beginnings and ends of the lines of each block had not seemingly suffered extensive damage and abrasion. But, with all this, there is so

[1] "At the northern extremity of the district of Zohâb is the little plain of Semîrâm, a natural fastness of the most extraordinary strength, which is formed by a range of lofty and precipitous mountains extending in a semicircle from the river Diyâlah, here called the 'Abi-Shirwân, and enclosing an area of about eight miles in length and four in breadth." . . . "I searched eagerly for ancient monuments, and though I failed to discover any in the plain itself, yet across the river, at a distance of about three farsakhs, on the road to Suleïmâníyah, I heard of sculptures and statues which would well merit the attention of any future traveller in this country. The place is called Pá'ikal'ah, the foot of the castle, or But Khânah, the idol temple."—Rawlinson, Jour. R. Geog. Soc., ix. pp. 28–30.

much to excite interest in the broken sections we are already in possession of, that I confidently make the appeal to those who may happen to be in a position to improve our existing copies by means of photography, impressions, rubbings, new hand-tracings, or, better still, by intelligent transcripts in modern Pehlvi—for aid in the cause, towards which the portions of the text, now printed, will contribute something in the way of a first proof, and for the encouragement otherwise of future Palæographers, we may hope that, under a closer examination, the duplicate legends may aid each other both in defective passages and in the correction of the present disjointed order of sequence: while, as the first investigation was necessarily hasty, new discoveries of materials may happily reward more deliberate explorers, even as we can now appeal to the immense advance upon the imperfect transcripts of Niebuhr and Morier, achieved by the less hurried and amplified facsimiles of M.M. Flandin and Coste.[1]

In order to bring the entire subject under one view, I have collected together all the fragmentary inscriptions of the Sassanidæ at present known, commencing with those interpreted by De Sacy, which I simply reproduce in their corresponding literal equivalents in modern Hebrew and Persian type. The same course has been pursued with the highly interesting bilingual inscription of Sapor, from Hájíábád. Sir H. Rawlinson's unpublished copies of the Pái Kúlí legends, as well as his improved transcripts of the Ṭák-i-Bustán epigraphs have, however, been more exactly imitated in modern Pehlvi type, which has been made so far competent to resume its primitive duty by the introduction of three letters of the earlier alphabet, which have been lost in the degraded writing of the extant MSS., and finally a similar plan has been followed in the representation of the legible portions of two long and, for the present, most tantalizing inscriptions of Sapor: artists' designs of which have

[1] Ker Porter remarks (i. p. 574), M. de Sacy "has followed Niebuhr's copy, which, strange to say, having been made so many years anterior to mine, exhibits an inscription much more defaced than I found it. This may be seen by comparing the large letters in my copy on the drawing with the large letters in M. de Sacy's Greek transcript." [Mem. sur div Ant. p. 31].

been given in Flandin's great work,[1] though I am not aware that any attempt has hitherto been made to decipher or explain these singularly comprehensive documents. I am indebted to the same publication for the unique inscription of Narses, at Sháhpúr, which, together with the legends from the Royal signets of Varahrán *Kirmán Sháh* have equally been admitted to the honours of the adapted semblance of their contemporary Pehlvi.

None of the original drawings or published engravings of the more important inscriptions are sufficiently exact or continuously complete to recommend them for imitation in *facsimile* engravings, and even the plaster-casts from Hájíábád, however well they reproduce portions of the associate inscriptions, as exhibited in the Photograph, would not, in their present state, suffice to form an unbroken or perfect copy. The expedient has therefore been again adopted of recognizing these absolute impressions from the sculptured rock as a basis for the construction of standard alphabets of either class. In each case, the best examples of the normal character have been selected from the often-varying outlines of the same letter as fashioned by the local mason, and regard has always been paid to the corresponding outline of the given letter in other monuments of the period, whether lapidary, numismatic, or sigillary. The result has been embodied in the double column of alphabets engraved on wood, arranged with the ordinary type in the accompanying table; and, as in the absence of all other positive examples of lapidary writing, these letters have to play a conspicuous part as representative types of their several palæographic systems, no effort, short of cutting the individual letters, has been spared on my part to secure a true and effective rendering of the special characteristics of each symbol.

The primary derivation of these alphabets may obviously be traced to Phœnico-Babylonian teachings. Specimens of that form of writing occur, so to say, *in situ*, as early as the time

[1] Voyage en Perse, M. M. Eugène Flandin et Paul Coste, entrepris par ordre de M. le Ministre des Affaires Étrangères. D'après les instructions dressées par l'Institut. Paris, 1851. 6 vols. folio, plates, etc., and 2 vols. 8vo. text.

of Sargon, B.C. 721, when the individual characters present themselves in a fixed and cultivated form, far removed from the early stages of crude invention, an indication that, apart from the almost simultaneously established geographical range of cognate letters, would claim for them an extended anterior currency, which it would be as difficult to limit as to define; my own impressions have always leant towards the concession of a far earlier development of that division of national civilization, which is comprised in the "art of writing," than the majority of Palæographers are prepared to recognize. Let Hieroglyphics and Cuneiform retain their ancient fame; but the question succeeds, as to how close upon their earliest traces did other systems of writing assert themselves, more facile in materials and more suitable for the purposes of commercial and private life than the formal sculptured figures of the Egyptian temples, or the complicated arrow-headed syllabary of Mesopotamian Palaces, which latter mechanism, however, in its transitional variations, so firmly retained popular favour in virtue of its applicability to the ever-ready clay, the comparative indestructibility of which had been established by many ages of local use.[1]

Egyptologers, on their part, concede a very archaic date for the use of parallel systems of writing, and the age of Phœnician, with our present information, need no longer be narrowed within the limits defined by its surviving monuments, the majority of which must be held to have disappeared with the perishable material chiefly used for their reception. It it is clear that some form of Phœnician, constituting a kind of current hand, was in official use under the Assyrian kings, as the authoritative definition of the lion-weights in the letters of that alphabet sufficiently declares; and we are further justified in assuming, in all cases where two Scribes are represented in the royal sculptures, that in intentional contrast to the Cuneiform manipulator, the second amanuensis, who uses a reed and a parchment

[1] Rawlinson, J.R.A.S. x, pp. 32, 340, and vol. i. N.S. p. 245. See also the names of Seleucus Philopater (187–175 B.C.), Antiochus (175–164 B.C.), and Demetrius (146–139 B.C.), upon the Cuneiform tablets of terra-cotta in the British Museum, deciphered by Oppert, "Expédition en Mésopotamie," ii. 367.

roll, is designed to portray a man writing with ink in some one of the, as yet, but slightly divergent provincialisms of archaic Phœnician.

Sargon's Record Chamber has already proved itself a perfect storehouse of palæographic data, and, if I am not mistaken, may claim to add another to its list of contemporary alphabets. Mr. Layard, in his admirable description of his own discoveries at Koyunjuk, interested his readers in an unusual degree by an account of the still surviving association of the hieroglyphic signet of Subaco, with that of the Assyrian king on a lump of clay, which was supposed to have formed the connecting attestation of the less permanent substance upon which some royal treaty or compact had been engrossed. In the same closet were found several impressions of smaller seals on suitably-sized bits of clay, which at the time attracted no attention; these, however, on closer scrutiny, seem to bear four varying letters, which can scarcely represent anything but ancient Ethiopian characters; at least two, if not three out of the four letters are readily identifiable with certain corresponding characters of the modern alphabets.[1] It is not necessary, for the purpose of proving the currency of this form of writing, that we should be able to detect any of the leading names, either of Subaco, his relatives, or ministers. The importance of the identification consists in the very unexpected determination of the definite antiquity of the writing of the Ethiopian and cognate nationalities, and the very close bearing this date has upon the alphabetical schemes of the

[1] Mr. Layard's account of the discovery of these seals is as follows:—"In a chamber or passage [leading into the archive chamber] in the south-west corner of the palace of Kouyunjik, were found a large number of pieces of fine clay bearing the impressions of seals, which, there is no doubt, had been affixed, like modern official seals of wax, to documents written on leather, papyrus, or parchment. Such documents, with seals of clay still attached, have been discovered in Egypt, and specimens are still preserved in the British Museum. The writings themselves have been consumed by the fire which destroyed the building or had perished from decay. In the stamped clay, however, may still be seen the holes for the string or strips of skin by which the seal was fastened; in some instances the ashes of the string itself remain, with the marks of the fingers and thumb. The greater part of these seals are Assyrian; but with them are others bearing Egyptian, Phœnician, and doubtful symbols and characters. But the most remarkable and important of the Egyptain seals are two impressions of a royal signet, which, though imperfect, retain the cartouche, with the name of the king, so as to be perfectly legible. It is one well known to Egyptian scholars as that of the second Sabaco, the Æthiopian of the twenty-fifth dynasty. On the same

Indian Ethiopians,[1] and the kindred nations to the south-eastward, in which many points of constructive identity have already been recognized.

piece of clay is impressed an Assyrian seal, with a device representing a priest ministering before the king, probably a royal signet."

The annexed woodcut outlines represent six of the Ethiopian seals, copied from the extant clay-impressions of the original signets, that have survived both "Nineveh and Babylon." My object in this, and I trust in all similar cases, is not to force

1 2 3 4 5 6 7

identities, but to place before my fellow labourers coincidences that may perchance elicit new truths. It is not pretended that the literal symbols here found associated with Egyptian hieroglyphics and Assyrian cuneiform will tally or accord exactly with the transmutations incident to the alphabetical developments of the once powerful, but for many centuries obscure, nationalities that in the interval must have remained more than ordinarily indebted to the advancing world around them. Under this latitude of identification, we may freely appeal to the later forms of Ethiopic, Amharic, or other cognate conservators of traces of the ancient writing, though it is more to the general palæographic configuration than to absolute and complete uniformity of outline that any test must be applied.

It may be said in regard to the seals now presented, that they convey in all but five independent letters; the most marked of the number is the , which occurs with sufficient clearness on three occasions. There can be little hesitation in associating this form with the modern Himyaritic *sh* or the Ethiopian *shă*, especially when the subjunct vowel *i* is added, which is so distinctly seen in a varied form, even under possible repetition, in the ancient example.

The second figure of special mark is the , which offers a more dubious range of identification among the derivative Ethiopian forms of *hi*, *hé*, extending even to the Amharic *khă*, and many other possible renderings; but the most curious coincidence is in the near connection of the sign with the Sanskrit of Northern India (Prinsep's Essays, ii. p. 40, pl. xxxviii.).

The third character, which almost seems to have been in a transition stage at the time these seals were fashioned, may be reduced in the modern alphabets to the Ethiopian *tă* or *wă*; but of the prevailing coincidences of formation under the general Ethiopian scheme there can be little question.

The imperfect outline , which recurs on four occasions, may be an Amharic *jă*, or other consonantal combination of *j*, with a different vowel: an approximate likeness is also to be detected in the Coptic *j*; or the old figure may, perchance, constitute the prototype of the modern Himyaritic *m*.

[1] Herodotus, ii. 94; vii. 70. Rawlinson's Herodotus, vol. i. 450; iii. 264, note 1; iv. p. 320. J. R. A. S. xv. 233.

The career of Phœnician writing in Mesopotamia and the proximate provinces of Western Persia, during the nine centuries and a half intervening between the reigns of Sargon and Ardeshir Bábekán, can only be obscurely traced. We know that the same twenty-two letters, which fulfilled their foreign mission in the creation of the alphabets of Greece and Rome, penetrated but little changed in their normal forms to the pillars of Hercules; while in the opposite direction, under the treatment of the Vedic Aryans, they constituted the basis of an elaborate alphabet of forty-nine signs, the date of whose adaptation is unascertained, but which has now been discovered to have attained full and complete development from Bactria up to the banks of the Jumna, in 250 B.C.[1] How the original alphabet matured its literal forms nearer home we are not in a condition to determine;[2] there is little doubt but that Cuneiform writing on its part maintained its position in official and commercial documents for a far longer period than might have been anticipated, but whether this extended vitality was due to the improved intelligence of professional scribes, to its superior accuracy of definition as compared with the limited scope of Phœnician,[3] or to the more material question of the cheapness and durability of the clay, whose surface, on the

[1] Prinsep's Essays, ii. 114; Journ. R. A. S. vol. i. N.S. p. 468; Numismatic Chronicle, vol. iii. N.S. (1863) pp. 229, 235, "Bactrian Alphabet."

[2] M. de Vogüé has given us a comprehensive *résumé* of the progress of Phœnician writing to the westward, which I quote in his own words:—"1. Antérieurement au VIe siècle, l'alphabet commun à toutes les populations sémitiques de la Syrie est l'alphabet phénicien archaïque, souche de l'écriture grecque et de tous les systèmes graphiques de l'occident. 2. Vers le VIe siècle, l'écriture phénicienne type, celle que j'ai appelée *Sidonienne*, se constitue définitivement: le plus beau monument de cette écriture est le célèbre sarcophage d'Esmunazar; en même temps la branche araméenne se sépare de la souche commune. Le caractère principal de ce nouvel alphabet est l'ouverture des boucles des lettres *beth*, *daleth*, *aïn*, *resch*. Mais pendant deux siècles environ, à côté de ces formes nouvelles se maintient un certain nombre de formes anciennes; l'altération de toutes les lettres n'est pas simultanée, de sorte que l'alphabet conserve un caractère mixte qui m'a conduit à lui donner le nom d'Araméo-Phénicien. Le meilleur exemple de cette écriture est l'inscription du Lion d'Abydos. 3. Vers la fin du V. siècle, l'alphabet araméen se constitue définitivement sur les pierres gravées, sur les médailles des satrapes de l'Asie mineure." Rev. Arch. ix. (1864), p. 204.

[3] M. Oppert makes some interesting remarks upon this subject; among the rest, "L'épigraphie assyrienne, d'ailleurs, malgré les complications inhérentes à l'écriture anarienne, a un avantage précieux sur l'épigraphie des autres peuples sémitiques. Les mots y sont séparés et les voyelles sont exprimées, ce qui constitue un avantage encore plus important pour l'interprète des textes."—Journal Asiatique, 1863, p. 478.

other hand, was so eminently unfitted for the reception of the curved lines of the latter, we need not now stop to enquire.

Many incidental examples of the local Phœnico-Babylonian of various epochs are to be found associated with the concurrent Cuneiform on the clay tablets described by Sir H. Rawlinson (B.C. 700–500).[1]

Towards the westward the Persian Satraps of the Achæmenidæ employed the indigenous Phœnician,[2] and anonymous Darics, presumably of the Great king, bear upon their surfaces the word מזדי in similar characters.[3]

But the earliest occasion upon which we can detect a tendency towards the identities and characteristics subsequently developed in the Chaldæo-Pehlvi is upon the coinage of Artaxias of Armenia, B.C. 189.[4] In this instance the letters ו, ג, י, ס, and ש notably depart from the style of the Phœnician of Sargon, and seem to have already assumed a near approach to the forms ultimately accepted as conventional in the alphabet reproduced in the woodcuts (p. 25). The peculiarities of this type of writing may afterwards be traced through the Armeno-Parthian coinages,[5] and irregularly on the Imperial Parthian mintages, both in silver and copper, dating from 113 A.D. up to the close of the dynasty.[6] These, with the casual appearance of some of the more marked Chaldæo-Pehlvi forms on the dubiously-classed money of Characene,[7] added to the odd juxtaposition of some of their special symbols with the local writing on the Kermán coins of Kodes (Kobád),[8] complete the list of examples at present known.

Of the fellow or Sassanian-Pehlvi alphabet no writing whatever has as yet been discovered prior to Ardeshír Bábekán,

[1] Journ. R. A. S. (new series), vol. i. pp. 187, 244.

[2] M. de Luynes "Essai sur la Numismatique des Satrapies et de la Phénicie. Paris, 1846.

[3] Gesenius, Pl. 36, fig. c.; Mionnet, Nos. 35, 36. Trésor de Numismatique, Pl. lxvi. figs. 1, 2.

[4] Numismatic Chronicle, xviii. 143; vol. vi. N.S. p. 245, and vii. 237.

[5] Numismatic Chronicle, vol. vi. N.S. 1866, note, p. 245.

[6] Numismatic Chronicle, xii. 68; xvii. 164; Lindsay, Coinage of Parthia, pl. iv. figs. 87, 89, 90, 93–96.

[7] Prinsep's Essays, i. 32.

[8] Numismatic Chronicle, iv. p. 220. (A new coin in the possession of General Cunningham gives the local name in full [illegible]).

with the exception of isolated letters, probably referring to local mints occasionally to be met with on the field of some of the Drachmas of the Parthians.[1]

The differences between the rival alphabets we are more immediately concerned with, will be seen to be rather constructive than fundamental; one leading theory evidently regulated the contrasted forms of the letters in each, the eventual divarications of the two systems, as in so many parallel cases, being due to the fortuitously most suitable and readily available material for the reception of the writing, which so often determined the ultimate method of graphic definition. The seemingly more archaic structure of the Chaldæo-Pehlvi clearly carried with it the reminiscence of Babylonian teachings, in which the formation of the letters was largely influenced by the obvious facilities of delineation. The ancient scribes of the Assyrian sculptures are represented as making use of a reed, or other description of pen, with which they wrote upon a flexible leather or parchment scroll, employing the indicator or, possibly, the first and second fingers of the left hand, to support the material at the point of contact of the pen in the ordinary line of writing; under these conditions the most obvious tendency would be towards down strokes, and thus it is found that almost every letter of Sargon's Phœnician consists primarily of a more or less perpendicular line, the minor discriminations being effected by side strokes more varied in construction but of less thickness and prominence; as time went on, the practice developed itself of forming as many letters as possible after one and the same process of manipulation, the essential difference between the characters being marked by scarcely perceptible variations in the leading design; hence arose the perplexing result of the general sameness and uniformity, and consequent difficulty of recognition of the imperfectly contrasted letters so marked in Chaldæo-Pehlvi, and still so troublesome in modern Hebrew.

The course followed by the pen in the Chaldæo-Pehlvi

[1] Parthian coin of Sanabares, dated 313 (A.D. 2), in the British Museum, with a Parthian D [illegible] and a Sassanian [illegible] on the obverse field. See also Numismatic Chronicle, xvii. 169; Lindsay, pl. xi. Arsaces XXX.

caligraphy was singularly repetitive, starting from a given point at the top of the line of writing, it proceeded slightly downwards with a backward sweep, more or less prolonged; from this angle the characteristic perpendicular curve commenced, to be supplemented by the concluding turn of the pen which so often constituted the effective definition of the value of the letter. This formation is followed in the letters ב, ך, כ, and less obviously in ג. The letters ח, ם, and ס commence with similar leading lines, but have discriminating marks added by a second application of the pen; in like manner ך is distinguished from ר by a separate foot crescent, a sign which finds its parallel in the dot of the Syriac ܕ. The remaining letters also had much in common, but in these instances the initial point of the character was thrown slightly backwards on the head-line of the writing, and the down-stroke proceeded more abruptly, finishing with a minute and nearly uniform curve to the left; under this heading may be classed the simple forms ׳ and ז, and the combined outlines ם, ת, ש, ל (כ), ה, and ״. Even the letter א probably consisted originally of an inclined duplication of the ׳, with a prolonged foot-line connecting the two down-strokes. The single exception to the descending curves is afforded by the letter ו, which must be supposed to have been constructed like the upward arch of the associate ת, which in the Syriac *waw* grew into a round ܘ, the Chaldæo-Pehlvi form of which, passing through the Sassanian 2, finally settled itself into the Arabic و.

The variation in the configuration of the letters of the Sassanian Pehlvi, as compared with its fellow alphabet of more determined Semitic aspect, may be attributed to the simple action of a different method of manipulation, involving a less restrained movement of the hand, and greater freedom in the onward or backward sweep of the pen than was compatible with the conventional restrictions of the caligraphy of Western Asia. There is every reason to believe that the ancient races to the east of the Tigris, in common with the partially civilized populations ranging over Central Asia and the Himalayas, very early in the world's history, appreciated the utility of birch-bark, and, even in the infancy of letters,[1] its applicability to the purposes of writing would readily have suggested itself. At all events, we have direct and independent evidence of its use in Afghânistan some centuries B.C.,[2] and we can cite very credible and unconstrained testimony to the fact that much of the sacred literature of the Ancient Persians was engrossed upon this substance,[3] con-

[1] To show how forms of writing in early times must have been determined by circumstances and accessible materials, it may be noted that even so late as the days of Muhammad, when there were civilized teachers from the many nations around them, the Arabs had still to engross the stray sayings of their Prophet upon stones and other strange and readily available substances. Sir Wm. Muir tells us, "after each passage was recited by Muhammad before the Companions or followers who happened to be present, it was generally committed to writing by some one amongst them upon palm-leaves, leather, stones, or such other rude material as conveniently came to hand." Life of Mahomet. London, 1861. Vol. i. p. iii.—Dr. Sprenger, in his Life of the Prophet (German edit. Berlin, 1865, iii. p. xxxix.), enumerates leather and parchment, slate, palm-leaves, camel's shoulder-blades. Said's copy was written on leaves of palm or on scrolls and papyrus.

[2] H. H. Wilson. *Ariana Antiqua*, pp. 59, 60, 83, 84, 94, 106-7, 111.

[3] I am quite aware that tradition affirms that the substance employed was 12,000 "Cow-skins" or parchments (Masudi, French edition, ii. p. 125. Hyde de relig. vet. Persar. 318), which might be understood as perfectly consistent with all the probabilities if it were admitted that, of the two copies of the sacred books mentioned in the subjoined extract from the Dinkard, the one deposited at Persepolis and the other at Ispahân, that the former was written in the Chaldæo-Pehlvi on skins, and the latter in the corresponding alphabet on birch-bark.

The following passages from the Dinkard, lately published by Dr. Haug, relating to the original collection, destruction, and subsequent attempts at the recovery of the sacred writings of the Zoroastrians are of sufficient interest, both historically and geographically, to claim a notice in this place. This portion of the Pehlvi text is admitted to have been added and incorporated only on the final rearrangement of the scattered materials of the ancient books. Nor does Dr. Haug himself seem quite satisfied with his own interpretation, which, considering the degraded character of the text, is scarcely to be wondered at.

1. "The book 'Dinkard' is a book on the religion, that people may obtain (a knowledge of) the good religion. The book 'Dinkard' has been compiled from all the knowledge acquired (to be) a publication of the Mazdayasnian (Zoroastrian) religion. 2. It was at first made by the first disciples of the prophet Zertusht Sapetman. . . . . . 3. The excellent king Kai Vishtâsp ordered to write down the information on each subject, according to the original information, embracing the original questions and answers, and deposited them, from the first to the last, in the treasury of Shaspigân ("Pasargadae," Haug). He also issued orders to spread copies (of the original). 4. Of these he sent afterwards one to the castle (where) written documents (were preserved), that the knowledge might be kept there. 5. During the destruction of the Irânian town (Persepolis. The *dezh-i-nipisht* is supposed to have been the library of that metropolis.—Haug) by the unlucky robber Alexander [الکسندر] after it had come into his possession, that (copy which was) in the castle (where) written documents (were kept) was burnt. The other which was in the treasury of Shaspigân fell into the hands of the Romans [اروماپان] (Greeks). From it a Grecian [یوناییک] translation was made that the sayings of antiquity might become known. 6. 7. Ardeshir Bâbekân, the king of kings [اوتاشتر مرکان مرکا پاپکان]

siderable remains of which, indeed, preserved with unusual care, were discovered at Isfahán by the Arabs in A.D. 961.[1] This material, while it would on the one hand, in its smooth surface, offer ample facilities for the unchecked flow of the

appeared. He came to restore the Iránian empire; he collected all the writings from the various places were they were scattered. . . . It (the Dinkart) was then (thus) restored, and made just as perfect as the original light (copy) which had been kept in the treasury of Shapiá ('Shapigân'—Haug) [= اصفهان]." See extract from Hamza, note 1, below.]

"The beginning of the Ardâi Virâf Nâmah" (from two Pahlavi MSS.).

1. "It is thus reported that after the religion had been received and established by the holy Zertosht, it was up to the completion of 300 years in its purity, and men were without doubts (there were no heresies). 2. After (that time) the evil spirit, the devil, the impious, instigated, in order to make man doubt the truth of religion, the wicked Alexander, the Roman [اركسكندر اروماياكث], residing in *Mudiras* (Egypt) that he came to wage a heavy fight and war against the Iránian country. 3. He killed the ruler of Irán, destroyed the residence [بيا] and empire, and laid it waste. 4. And the religious books, that is, the whole Avesta and Zand, which were written on prepared cow-skins with gold ink, were deposited at Istakhr Bâbegân, in the fort of the library. But Ahraman, the evil-doer, brought Alexander, the Roman, who resided in Egypt, that he burnt (the books), and killed the Dasturs, the Judges, the Herbads, the Mobeds," etc. [چند دستوبران و داتوبران و هيربدان و مگوپتان]. "An old Zand-Pahlavi Glossary, or the "Farhang-i-oim yak," the original Fahlvi work upon which Anquetil's vocabulary was based, edited by Hoshengji Jamaspji, and printed under the supervision of Dr. Martin Haug. Stuttgart, 1867."

[1] Hamza Isfaháni (obiit, A.H. 350, A.D. 961) gives an interesting narrative of the discovery of certain ancient Persian archives, written on birch-bark. I quote the substance of the passage in the Latin translation of Dr. Gottwaldt—Anno cum. (A.D. 961), latus ejus aedificii quod Saraveih nominatur atque intra urbem Djei (Isfahán) situm est, corruit et domum retexit, in qua fere L utres erant, e corio confecti atque inscripti literis, quales antea nemo viderat. Quando ibi depositi fuissent, ignotum erat. Cum [illegible] a me s[illegible]tum esset, quae de mirabili illo aedificio scirem, hominibus promsi librum Abu Mascharis, astrologi Balchensis, cujus nomen est: Liber de diversitate Tabularum astronomicarum. Ibi ille: Reges (Persarum), inquit, tanto studio tenebantur disciplinas conservandi, tanta cupiditate eas per omne aevum perpetuandi, tanta sollicitudine eas ab injuriis aëris et humi defendendi, ut iis inter materias scriptorias eam eligerent, quae illas injurias optime ferret, vetustati diutissime resisteret ac mucori et obliterationi minime obnoxia esset, id est, librum (corticem interiorem) fagi, qui liber vocatur túz. Hoc exemplum imitati Seres et Indi atque populi iis finitimi ad arcus, quibus ad sagitandum utuntur . . . . . Ad arcem igitur, quae nunc intra Djei sita est, profecti ibi disciplinas deposuerunt. Illud aedificium, nomine Saraveih, ad nostra usque tempora perduravit; atque ex eo ipso cognitum est, quis id condiderit, propterea quod abhinc multos annos latere ejus aedificii collapso camera in conspectum venit, ex argilla secta constructa, ubi multi majorum libri inventi sunt, in quibus depositae erant variae eorum disciplinae, omnes lingua persica antiqua scripti in cortice túz. Hamzae Ispahanensis (Annalium Libri, x. pp. 162, xxv.) St Petersbourg, 1844.—Abú Rihán Al Birúní (circâ 940 A.D.) also records: Mais dans les provinces du centre et du nord de l'Inde, on emploie l'écorce intérieure d'un arbre appelé *touz* [توز] C'est avec l'écorce d'un arbre du même genre qu'on recouvre les arcs; celle-ci se nomme *boudj* [بهوج] (Bhúrjja). Renaud, Mem. sur l'Inde, p. 305. See also Prinsep's Essays, ii. 45.

pen, would, in the extreme tenuity of its texture, demand some more equable and uniform support than the primitive expedient of extended forefingers: and, as improved appliances were enlisted in its cause, it may have come to be held in deserved favour, especially when its other merits, so gravely enlarged upon by the local annalist, are taken into consideration. Certain it is that to this day, among the Bhoteahs and other natives of the Himalaya, birch-bark maintains its ancient uses, and many a petition and other documents engrossed on its surface find their way among the "stamped papers" and the like civilized records of the Courts of the British Government in those mountains. It is then to the enhanced freedom of penmanship incident to the employment of birch-bark that I am disposed to attribute the leading peculiarities of this style of writing. The material in question secured to the amanuensis an unchecked power of forming curves and an unrestrained action of the pen in any given direction; but its ultimate effect upon the identity of the Sassanian character was mainly due to the gift of continuous onward movement in the line of writing, which eventually developed itself into the Kufic scheme, where a single line drawn from right to left constituted the basis of the entire alphabet in its conjunct form,[1] and the innate contrast between the two styles of writing maintains itself to the last, and may be detected at the present day in the pervading descending stroke of the Hebrew finals, and in the prolonged sweep, in the general line of writing, of certain Arabic terminal letters; while, under the larger and more comprehensive view of the same question, we may trace in the contrasted formation and relative location of the short vowels, a practical and conclusive illustration of the original caligraphic type of either system.

The ruling ideal of this Pehlvi scheme of writing proceeded upon a groundwork of curves, the leading model of which declares itself in the letter ℓ, which commenced towards the top of the general line of writing, being extended slightly upward and continued backwards and downwards,

[1] I do not know whether the singular identity of the employment of a central leading-line, in our own Oghams, has as yet been the subject of notice.

after the fashion of a reversed Roman C. This formation enters more or less into the composition of the letters ت, چ, د, ر, س, ش, ک, ل, م, و, *i*, and *ī long*. In process of time, as the writing became more cursive, the initial point of the *i*, and of those letters which more immediately followed its tracing, was thrown higher up and further back in the ordinary line, while the concluding turn of the curve was prolonged and occasionally run into other letters. The single character in this alphabetical series that was discriminated in its *final* form, from its normal initial or medial representative, was the short *i*; and the manner in which this was effected would almost imply that it was intended in the very act to check the onward flow of the writing in the way of an upward stop, as the final was made to commence even below the middle of the horizontal line of letters and the concluding point of the three-quarters of a circle was not allowed to reach the ordinary foot lines [].

It remains for me to notice more particularly a few of the letters of either alphabet with reference to their derivation and values, and their relative bearing upon the corresponding signs of other systems. First in order presents itself the independently-organized symbol for *ch*, a letter of considerable importance in Aryan tongues, but which the Greeks and Romans, in servilely following Semitic originals, so strangely failed to provide a literal representative for. The Chaldæo-Pehlvi contented itself with a like deficiency, and supplied the place of the *ch* by *sh*. The Sassanian character  *ch* was clearly based upon the  *h* of its own alphabetical scheme, the additional power being given by the foot-stroke backwards, which was one of the leading peculiarities of this style of writing. The letter in its adapted form bears a faint, but not impossibly an intentional, resemblance to the Bactrian  *ch*.

The Sassanian alphabet, again, is itself defective in the Semitic aspirate ח *kh*, which the Greeks converted into *H*, a sound that fell short of the compound  *hu* in Sassanian, which was, perhaps, the best equivalent that the latter writing admitted of. It is to be remarked that, in spite of Indian influences, the Bactrian *kh* itself did not, for some time, assume a very definite or constant form.[1]

The greatest obstacle, without any exception, to a satisfactory and positive interpretation of the early Sassanian inscriptions is incident to the inconvenient identity of the sign which has to answer for the sounds both of *r* and *w*. The Chaldæo-Pehlvi forms of [glyph] *r* and [glyph] *w*, like the Bactrian [glyph] *r* and [glyph] *v*, have something in common, and the association survives in the modern Hebrew ר, ו; but in all these cases there is a distinct, though not very marked, means of discrimination. Whereas, in the Sassanian-Pehlvi, there is not only no aid to the determination of whether the symbol 2 stands for ر or و; but in many cases, where it is clearly the former, it has often to be read by the light of modern interpretation, as ل. Moreover, whenever two of these signs occur together, thus 22 they present all the above alternatives, and, in addition, may chance to represent an oft-recurring malformation of the letter [glyph] due either to imperfect execution in the original, or, more frequently, to faulty copying by the modern draftsman; but in some cases the double 22 constitutes the authorised and constant formation of the ش, altogether apart from any possible errors of original designers, contemporary engravers, or travellers from the West, who have in later days made these inscriptions known to us. The alphabet had not yet arrived at the equally perplexing transformation whereby the letters W and N came to hold a single literal representative in common in the [glyph] = W and [glyph] = N of the Arabico-Pehlvi coins and modern MSS. writing;[2] but this latter, the "grand Schiboleth du Pehlvie" of Joseph Müller,[3] is far

[1] Prinsep's Essays, ii. 147.

[2] The eventual complication or conglomeration of signs under which the 2 = و fell into community and association with the symbol [glyph], the ancient ن, is still an enigma; but as it does not come within the range of the writing of the Sassanian Inscriptions, I commend it to the attention of those who still find a difficulty in reconciling the Parsi "Ashema" with the proper Ashârma of earlier date. (See, for instance, Olm Yak, p. xxvii.)

[3] Journal Asiatique, 1839. "Essai sur la langue Pehlvie." J.R.A.S. xii. 269.

less obstructive in practice than the earlier association of R and W. In order to meet this peculiarity in the Sassanian writing, I have had the letter ב cut in *fac-simile* and prepared for use with the modern Pehlvi type.

The s of the joint alphabets demands a passing comment, as in its near identity in both systems, and the complete dissimilarity of either outline to any archaic or other derivative form of the letter in Phœnician, it would seem that its origin must be sought for elsewhere; it is singular that the Bactrian symbol for ṣ ꟸ in 250 B.C. ⊓ (in Aryan Indian ⋒), and the Armenian correspondent of s Ս in B.C. 189, should so nearly accord, and that their general formation should be preserved so completely in the Pehlvi alphabets of the Sassanians. The following are the gradational representatives of each class ח ד ח ה. The concluding example is taken from the Sassanian section of the Hájíábád sculpture, and its configuration is aptly illustrative of the method in which the normal letter was formed, namely, by a second application of the pen to the leading design. In the present instance the body of the character is composed of the often-recurring ו with a reduced ו supplemented to it. The accelerated penmanship of more practised scribes gradually transformed the letter first into ꝏ and eventually into ڛ and ڛـ, whence it finally progressed into the Pehlvi ، the Zend ، and the Arabic س.

I have still to advert to two very serious difficulties in the decipherment of these alphabets; the one dependent upon the great similarity existing between the signs for R and Z in the Chaldæo-Pehlvi, which often renders them hopelessly indistinguishable; this is the case even in the positive reproduction of the inscription at Hájíábád, so it may be imagined what amount of reliance is to be placed upon the drawings of mere copyists. As a general rule the letter R is simple and direct in its downward course, while the Z is more curved in its sweep, and more marked in the initial and final points.

The second obstruction to assured interpretation consists more in the oral sound to be attributed to the several letters ב = R and ל = L in the Sassanian writing. At times it would seem that these letters were knowingly used indifferently; on other occasions ignorance of or insensibility to the true force of the Semitic ל may have prevailed; though in some instances, again, discrimination in their contrasted employment is evident, especially in words in which a complication already exists, arising out of the community of the sounds of B and W inherent in their common sign ב.[1] If, in addition to these constructive difficulties, we add the imperfect phonetic aptitude or the want of system in the use of the symbols for د-D and ت-T, گ-G and ک-K; and more important than all, the authorised dialectic interchange of ب B, پ P (ف F), and و W, we have offered a goodly list of reasons why European interpreters have made such scant progress in Pehlvi readings.

One of the most curious questions in the whole range of this enquiry is presented in the history of that strangely influential vowel in the Persian tongue, the letter *i*; we have already seen the important part played by the normal form of that character in the supplementary definition of the concurrent signs of the Chaldæo-Pehlvi, and attention has been drawn to a somewhat parallel fundamental influence exercised by the typical curve of the Sassanian *i*, among the other letters of its own alphabet; it is further clear that neither of the very differently-fashioned letters of the joint Pehlvi systems of writing can be referred to corresponding Semitic originals as the latter are ordinarily determined; all of which adhere with more or less fidelity to a vague reminiscence of the archaic 𐤉. A singular evidence of the community of Aryanism in alphabets suggests itself in these facts, though I am not prepared to claim any Noachian antiquity for the coincidence, but merely desire to show that the various branches of the Aryan pastoral races, as they are known to the modern world,[2] only began to understand and appreciate the value of

[1] مرکا and ملکا—فرمات and تیردت—فلمات and تیلدت. It is a curious fact that all the early Numismatic legends use ב both for B and W. ط does not appear till later, and then only irregularly. See J.R.A.S. xiii. 178.

[2] Report of the Meeting of the Royal Asiatic Society, 9th April, 1866; Athenæum, April, 1866; Numismatic Chronicle (1866) vol. vi. p. 172; Journal Asiatic Society of Bengal, July, 1866, p. 138.

the art of writing when they came into contact with urban populations in their own migatory advance and domestication among more civilized peoples, or when they achieved, in force, the conquest of earlier-settled nationalities. In this present case, at least, it is strange that the self-same leading idea should have prevailed throughout, in the adoption of the crude form of the vowel *i*, within a range that can be traced upwards from our own capital or italic *I*, through the Roman and Etruscan outline of the letter, and the independent Greek design,[1] whose but slightly modified shape is found typical in Armenia[2] some centuries B.C., and which re-appears almost identically in its normal tracing with our own matured result, in the Bactrian reconstruction, under Aryan treatment,[3] of the simple elements of the once *current* writing of Babylon.

The Sassanian alphabet manifestly incorporated the old Phœnician = *i* (the Persian Cuneiform)[4] into its own system, and as it was already in possession of an ordinary short I; the Semitic letter was devoted to the representation of the long or duplicated sound of that vowel.[5] A curious course

[1] The following forms of the Greek *iota* approach very closely to the Chaldæo-Pehlvi outline . See also Gesenius, pl. II.; Mionnet, volume "Planches," etc., 1808, pl. xxxi. Nos. 1, 2; "Inscriptiones Græcæ Vetustissimæ," H. G. Rose (Cambridge, 1825), table i. Nos. 11, 15, 16. etc.; "Corpus Inscriptionum Græcarum," A. Boeckh (Berlin, 1828), p. 6. "Sed imprimis insignis est litteræ Iota forma , quæ etiam in ære Petiliensi reperitur, et tum in nummis aliquot urbium Magnæ Græciæ, tum in nummo Gortyniorum, . . . derivata ex Oriente."—Swinton, Insc. Cit. Oxford, 1750.

[2] Coins of Artaxias, Numismatic Chronicle. October, 1867, No. 3 [|].

[3] The Bactrian medial *i* is composed of a single line thus /. In composition it crosses the body of the leading consonant. The initial *i* is formed by the addition of the sloping line to the short *a*, thus .—Numismatic Chronicle, N.S. iii. pl. vi.; Prinsep's Essays, ii. p. 161.

[4] There is some similarity of ideas in the form of the Pali I of Asoka's Inscriptions. Ex. gr. *gAI*, *gAī*.

[5] M. François Lenormant has devoted a lengthy article in the Journal Asiatique of Août-Septembre, 1865 (pp. 180–226), to "Études Paléographiques sur l'Alphabet Pahlevi, ses diverses variétés et son origine," in which he has done me the honour to quote largely from my first paper on Pehlvi writing which appeared in the twelfth volume of this Journal, 1849, as well as from a parallel notice on Arsacidan coins, etc., inserted in the Numismatic Chronicle of proximate date, without seemingly having been aware of the publication of my second contribution on the same subject, which was printed in our Journal for 1852 (vol. xiii. p. 373). M. Lenormant has not been altogether fortunate in the passages

attended the maturation of this literal sign in the parallel alphabet, which, though in the retention of its primitive forms, claiming so much more of a Semitic aspect, provided itself, from other sources, with a short *i*, and lost all trace of the proper Semitic ᛉ of Sargon's time, and hence had to invent anew the long *î* required for the due expression of the language it was eventually called upon to embody. The process by which this was effected is instructive, and may be said, in its

of my Essay which he has selected for adverse criticism,—a licence, however, I must confess he has been wisely chary of indulging in.

M. Le Normant is mistaken in supposing that Sir H. Rawlinson ever designed to insert a long א *âlef* in the word *Baga*, so that his over-officious attempt at correction, in this instance, proves altogether superfluous (J.R.A.S. x. pp. 93, 94, 187), but the implication, in the general run of the text, is, that I myself had attributed this error to Sir Henry, which I certainly never contemplated doing; nor, as far as I can gather from anything I have printed, did I give any colour for a supposition that I desired so to do (J.R.A.S. xii. 264; Numismatic Chronicle, xii. 74). Sir Henry undoubtedly suggested that the group of letters ordinarily following the king's titles in the Sassanian coin legends and inscriptions should be resolved into the letters *b. g.*, and hence he inferred, most correctly, that the term in question was *Baga*, divine (Sanskrit भग), supposing that, in the ordinary course of Aryan tongues, the several consonants optionally carried the inherent short vowel *a*. My correction merely extended to the separation of the character composing the second portion of the group into the since universally accepted *g. i.*

M. Lenormant has gone out of his way to assert that "Le savant anglais a prétendu, en effet, que le pehlevi ne possédait pas de ס." This is not quite an accurate statement of the case. If I had not recognised the existence and frequent use of an س, which letter duly appears in my alphabets (J.R.A.S. xii. pl. i.), I could have made but very little progress in Pehlvi decipherments. The question I did raise with regard to the origin of the earliest form of the Sassanian س (xii. 266), as found in the Hâjîâbâd sculptures, was not only perfectly legitimate and fairly and frankly stated, but there is even now no resisting the associate facts that the Chaldæo-Pehlvi version of Inscription No. vi. *infra*, makes use of the ז in the penultimate of סוריין, and that the corresponding س of the Sassanian text ᓂ is susceptible of being resolved into the typical elements of ᛉ. Moreover, it must be borne in mind that the Chaldæo-Pehlvi ס was still unidentified, though even then suggested the attribution which has since thrown new light upon the entire question (N.C. xii. 78). In short, the point of interest at that time was to determine the course and progress of the discrimination and graphic expression of the approximate sounds of *z* and *s* in the alphabets under discussion.

As regards my proposed rectification of M. De Sacy's סן in סבנין Bonsan, which M. Lenormant confidently designates as "inutilement contesté par M. Edward Thomas" (J.A. p. 193), I am sanguine that the ample data adduced below will satisfy more severe critics that the mistaken interpretation M. Lenormant insists upon sharing, in common with so many of Anquetil's ancient errors, may be safely left to find its own correction.

Finally, I am bound to place on record a distinct protest against the general accuracy of M. Lenormant's illustrative facsimiles. I imagined, in the first instance, that the French artist had reproduced in a crude and clumsy way the conscientious originals of the English engraver; but I see that M. Lenormant claims whatever credit is due upon that score for himself, in the declaration, "nous avons relevé nous-même les figures que nous donnons sur les plâtres offerts à la Société Asiatique de Londres par M. Rawlinson" (J.A. p. 188).

very mechanism, to add an independent proof of the true value attaching to the fellow character ـيم. The configuration of the ـيـ clearly proceeded upon the duplication of the simple or short *i* (ʃ); and in order to avoid the possible confusion of the new compound with the ordinary يـ a concluding curve was carried upwards and backwards from the second *i* through its own down-stroke and into the leading letter.

In course of time both these double letters disappear from public documents, but the Sassanian letter is preserved in the Parsi alphabet,[1] and is but little changed in its Zend form ۍ. While the short *i* was subjected to considerable modifications, till, on the Arabico-Pehlvi coins it appears as ـــ in its independent definition, or in the latest introductory stage towards the Naskhi "Kasrah-i-Izáfat."

As regards the true force of the fellow letters, though we may, for simplicity sake, designate them as long or double *i*'s, it is clear that the duty they had to perform in the less matured orthography of the third century A.D. will be represented by a very extended range of optional transcriptions when reduced into the elaborated characters of the present day, leaving the Chaldæo-Pehlvi letters to answer for their parallel power in the double יי. The Sassanian counterpart must clearly be admitted to stand, according to the context, for ى, يِ, ىٍ, ئ or ئي, and their several medial correspondents.

An apt illustration of the difficulty the limited characters of the Chaldæo-Pehlvi had to contend with in the definition of the mixed Aryan and Semitic speech they had to respond to, has lately been contributed, on the occasion of the natives of Persia having been called upon to reconstruct an alphabet suitable for the expression of their modern tongue out of the self-same literal elements they had abandoned so many con-

[1] Spiegel, Grammatik der Pârsisprache. Leipsig, 1851. I observe that Dr. Haug still adheres to the old lesson his Parsi instructors at Surat so erroneously taught Anquetil in 1760, and persists in interpreting the power of this letter as س. See preface to the "Farhang-i-oim yak," p. 21. Though he seems at one time (1862) to have been prepared to accept the reading of *ی*, converting the old 'Bouman' into '*Bary*.' "Sacred language of the Parsees," Bombay, 1862. p. 15.

turies ago. The motive for this experiment arose out of the desire of our Bible Society to furnish the Jewish converts in Persia with a version of the New Testament in the Hebrew character, with which they were already familiar, but textually couched in the spoken language of the country.[1] The subjoined table will show how this singular compromise was effected, and its details are of considerable value in the present inquiry, as giving us a clearer perception of how the modern ear was prepared to deal with the sounds of the actually current speech, and how, with a clear field and enlarged and matured powers of alphabetical development, those sounds were held to be critically defined and discriminated in the general reconstruction of the ancient alphabet.

HEBREW ALPHABET ADAPTED TO THE DEFINITION OF THE PERSIAN LANGUAGE.[2]

ا = א	خ = כ̇	ص = צ	ک = כ
ب = ב	د = ד	ض = צ̇	گ = ג
پ = פ	ذ = ד̇	ط = ט	ل = ל
ت = ת	ر = ר	ظ = ט̇	م = מ
ث = ת̇	ز = ז	ع = ע	ن = נ
ج = ג̇	ژ =	غ = ג̇	و = ו
چ = ג̈	س = ס	ف = פ̈	ه = ה
ح = ח	ش = ש	ق = ק	ی = י

א̄ = آ

One of the most curious results of this adaptive revival of the ancient letters is to prove to us, what I have already perseveringly contended for, that is, the use of some form of a double *i*, and some acknowledged method of writing such a compound with a view to avoid the possible confusion of the independant repetition of the short vowel, amid a series of letters in their nature so imperfectly discriminated *inter se*. Examples of

[1] The New Testament in question, designated "JUDÆO-PERSIC," was printed by Messrs. Harrison & Co. in 1847, under the editorship of Mr. E. Norris, from a text arranged by the natives of Persia according to their own perceptions of equivalent letters.

[2] Michaeli's Arabische Grammatik (Gott. 1781) arranged the discriminative marks as follows:— ת̄ = ت, ת̇ = ث, ח = ح, ג̄ = ج, כ̄ = خ, ד̄ = ذ, צ = ص, צ̄ = ض, ט = ط, ט̄ = ظ, ג̄ = غ, ק = ق, ה = ة.

such repetitions occur here in every page, as לויי, "a Levite," גאיי, "a place;" יעני יהודאי אסכריוטי, "namely, Judas Iscariot" (John xii. 3); בסויי ידיחו מי רפת, [he] "went towards Jericho." In its medial duplicate form it occurs in דר איין מושה, "in the law of Moses" (Luke xxiv. 44); but its most frequent appearance is in verbs, as מינמאיי, בגוייד, כשאייד, etc., where the introductory *y* is absolute. The *kasrah* form of the short *i* is expressed by the sign over the line, thus, יׄ, "he," דר באנה פדר מן, "in the house of my father" (John xiv. 2).

The comparative table of alphabets inserted below will, I trust, prove sufficiently explanatory in itself, though it may be needful to indicate the derivation of and authority for some of the less common forms. The excellent series of Numismatic Phœnician was cut for the Duc de Luynes, for the illustration of his work on the Satrapies. The outlines are chiefly derived from the forms of the Phœnician alphabet in use on the coins of Cilicia and Cyprus.

The old Syriac may be useful in the present instance among the associated Pehlvi alphabets for the purposes of comparison, in its near proximity in point of date and local employment. This font was prepared under the supervision of the late Dr. Cureton, whose account of the sources from whence it was derived is as follows:—

"It was principally copied from MSS. of the sixth century, and represents the earliest form of the character known to us. It is identical with that of the most ancient MS. in the British Museum—date A.D. 411; but the forms of the letters are made a little more carefully than they were written by the person who copied that MS., and imitate more closely those of some better scribe, although about a century later."

The modern Pehlvi was engraved by Marcellin Legrand of Paris, under the direct superintendence of M. Jules Mohl, and to my understanding offers the best and closest imitation of the ancient writing as yet produced. I have so far departed from the primary intention of the designers as to employ the letter *ꞔ*, to which they had assigned the value of a *kh*, as the more appropriate representative of the simple *h*, in order to avoid the confusion incident to the use of the unpointed *ꞔ*, which in the original scheme was called upon to do duty indifferently for either *a* or *h*.

PEHLVI ALPHABETS.

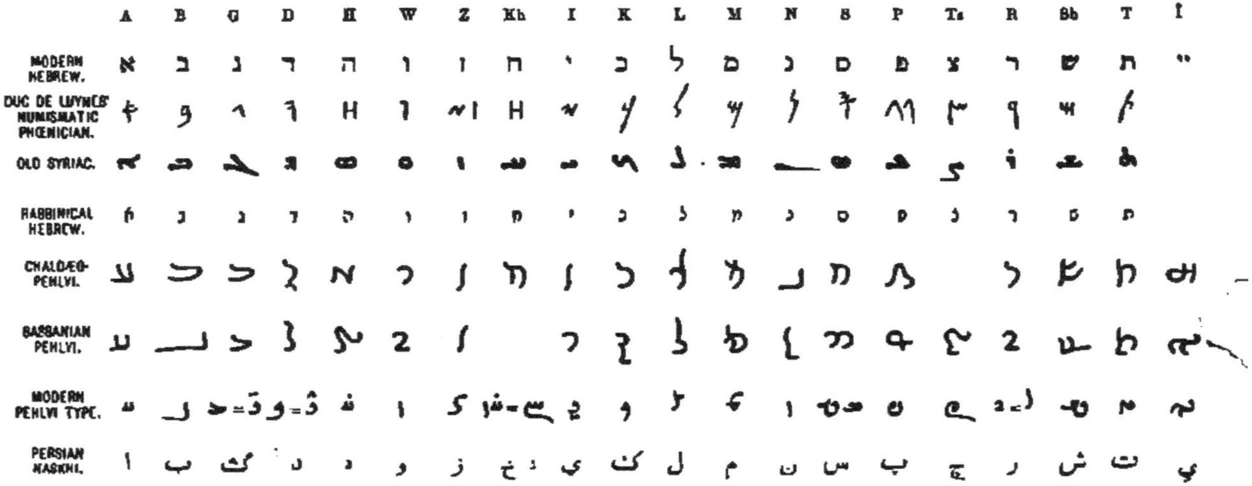

Hebrew Letters not used in the Pehlvi;—ט Teth = ; ע Ayin = ; ק Koph = ; צ Tsade, and ש Sin.

In order to complete the alphabetical illustrations connected with the later history of Sassanian writing, I append a comparative table of the Pehlvi and Zend characters, which in itself demonstrates the direct derivation of the latter series from its more crude model, and enables us to trace the amplification and elaboration of the earlier literal forms to meet the wants of the more refined grammar of the Zend, a reconstruction which seems to have been aided by the high degree of perfection already reached in the alphabetical definitions of cognate Aryan languages.

PEHLVI AND ZEND ALPHABETS.

VOWELS.

Short Vowels,	*Pehlvi,*	*a.*		*i.*	*u.*	
,,	*Zend,*	*a.*	*e.*	*i.*	*u.*	
Long Vowels,	*Pehlvi,*	*ai.*	*í.*			
,,	*Zend,*	*á.*	*í.*	*ú.*	*ê.*	*ē.*
,,	*Zend,*	*o.*	*ó.*	*ào.*		

CONSONANTS.

Gutturals,	*Pehlvi,*	*k.*	*hu.*		*g.*	
,,	*Zend,*	*k.*	*kh.*	*q.*	*g.*	*gh.*
Palatals,	*Pehlvi,*	*ch.*			*j.*	
,,	*Zend,*	*ch.*			*j.*	
Dentals,	*Pehlvi,*	*t.*			*d.*	
,,	*Zend,*	*t.*	*th.*	*th.*	*d.*	*dh.*
Labials,	*Pehlvi,*	*p.*			*b.*	
,,	*Zend,*	*p.*	*f.*		*b.*	
Semi-Vowels,	*Pehlvi,*	*i* or *y.*		*r.*		
,,	*Zend,*	(ɛ med.) *y.*		*r.*	(ɩ med.) *v.*	
,,	*Pehlvi,*	*v.* or *w.*		*h.*		
,,	*Zend,*	*w.*		*h.*		
Sibilants,	*Pehlvi,*	*s.*		*sh.*		*z.*
,,	*Zend,*	*s.* (*ç.*)	*sh.*	*s.*		*z.*
Nasals,	*Pehlvi,*	*n.*				*m.*
,,	*Zend,*	*n.*	*ñ.*	*an.*	*ṅ.*	*m.*

Inscription No. 1.

The first inscription of the series under review is engraved upon the most prominent of the Sassanian sculptures at Naksh-i-Rustam,[1] wherein Ormazd is represented as bestowing a second or Imperial cydaris upon Ardeshír Bábekán on the occasion of his final victory over the last of the Arsacidæ, whose prostrate body is exhibited on the battle field beneath the feet of the equestrian group, and whose individuality is distinctly marked by the snake-crested helmet of the Mede.[2] Ormazd's costume consists of a high mural crown, with closely twisted curls rising in a mass above it; his beard is cut square, and his flowing locks are curled elaborately over his shoulders, above and behind which float the conventional Sassanian fillets.[3] In his left hand he holds a sceptre or baton, erect, and with

[1] Ker Porter, vol. i. pl. xxiii. p. 548; Flandin, vol. iv. pl. 182. A similar sculpture, reproducing the same leading figures on foot, is copied in pl. xxvii. Ker Porter; Flandin, 192, 3.

[2] Astyages—اژدرها, "a dragon;" مار, "a serpent;" Moses of Khorene, i. 123, 167. *Hiê = Mar*, "serpent," Anquetil, ii. p. 497; Rawlinson, J.R.A.S. xv. 242; Zohak of the Sháh Námah, Haug, 157. अहि, "a serpent;" अहिजित्, a name of Krishna and Indra, "subduing a demon!" The Dahák of the Yasna is described as "tribus-oribus-præditum, tribus-capitibus," etc. (Kossowicz). Masaudi's tradition speaks of "deux serpents nés sur les épaules de Dahhak" (id. p. 252). Les descendans d'Astyages établis en Arménie portoient encore le nom de Vischabazouni ce que signifie *race de dragon*. Cette dénomination leur venoit du nom du roi des Mèdes.—St. Martin, i. 286.

[3] Flandin's copy, in plate 182 of his work, altogether omits these pennants, though Ormazd has them to the full in other plates, 186, 192 bis; (Ker Porter, xxvii. No. 1). Ormazd is frequently represented in other compositions amid these sculptures. For instance, in plate 44, Flandin, at Firozábád, where he again appears in the act of presenting a cydaris to Ardeshír. This bas relief is remarkable for the subsequent addition of a *modern* Pehlvi legend, which is only dubiously intelligible in Flandin's copy. Ormazd is depicted in a new and modified form in the bas-relief at Ták-i-Bustán (pl. lxvi. Ker Porter, vol. ii.; Malcolm's Persia, vol. i. p. 259; and pl. 14, Flandin, vol. i.), where he is introduced as apparently sanctioning the final abdication of Ardeshír and the transfer of the Sassanian diadem to Sapor.* Ormazd in this case stands at the back of the former monarch, with his feet resting on a lotus flower; he holds the peculiar baton or sceptre in the usual position, but this time with *both* hands; and instead of the hitherto unvarying mural crown, the head seems uncovered, but closely bound with the conventional diadem, with its broad pendant fillets, while the head itself is encircled with rays of glory, after the Western idea of a nimbus.†

* The association of Sapor in the government, or perhaps only his recognition as heir apparent, is illustrated by the coins of the period. See *Num. Chron.* xv. p. 181.

† A similar form is given to Ormazd's head-gear in the coin of Hormisdas II., quoted p. 43 *post*.

his right he extends towards the conqueror a circlet, to which are attached the broad wavy ribbons so exaggerated in their dimensions at this period.

Ardeshír wears a close-fitting scull-cap shaped helmet, from the centre of which ascends a globe-like balloon, which is supposed to typify some form of fire or other equivalent of our Western *halo*. The head-piece is encircled with a diadem, from which depend the Dynastic flowing fillets, and the helmet is completed for defensive purposes by cheek-plates and a sloping back-plate. The beard seems to have been injured if we are to trust Ker Porter's copy; but Flandin represents it as ending in a tied point, a fashion seemingly only introduced by Sapor. The hair is disarranged, possibly to indicate the recent combat. The remaining details of the sculpture are unimportant in their bearing upon the present inquiry, but it must be noted that the inscriptions, in either case, are cut upon the shoulder of the horse bearing the figure each of the triple legends are designed to indicate, so that there can be no possible doubt about the identification of the persons, or the intentional portraiture of the contrasted divinity and king; the former of which is of peculiar interest in disclosing the existing national ideal of the form and external attributes of Ormazd, so distinctly defined as "the god of the Arians" by Darius himself in his celebrated Cuneiform record at Behistun, iv. 12, 13 (J.R.A.S. xv. 130, 144).

The style of the legend embodying the monarch's titles, though tinged with ever-prevailing Oriental hyperbole, is modest in regard to the extent of his dominions, which are confined to *Irán* proper; and the like reserve is maintained in the epigraphs upon both Ardeshír's money, and many, if not all, of Sapor's coins;[1] though the inscriptions at Páï Kúlí, if they are found hereafter to have emanated from the founder of the dynasty, about which there may still be some vague doubt—would seem to prove that the *An Irán*, or countries other than *Irán*, in modern speech, associated as *Irán* and

[1] Varahran I. seems to have been the first to record the *An Irán* on his currency, but want of space in the field of the coins may well have counselled previous omissions.

Turán, had already been comprehended in Ardeshír's later conquests.

INSCRIPTION No. 1.—ARDESHÍR, BABEK, A.D. 226, at Naksh-i-Rustam.

I *is a transliteration, in modern Hebrew letters, of the original Chaldæo-Pehlvi Lapidary Text.*
II *is a transliteration, in modern Persian characters, of the associate Sassanian-Pehlvi Text.*
III *is a transcript of the original Greek translation, which is appended to the duplicate Oriental epigraphs.*

I. פתכר זניי מזדיזן אלהא ארתחשתר מלכין מלכא אריאן
II. پتكري زني مزديسن بگي ارتهشتر ملكان ملكا ايران
III.[1] ΤΟΥΤΟ ΤΟ ΠΡΟΣΩΠΟΝ ΜΑΣΔΑΣΝΟΥ ΘΕΟΥ ΑΡΤΑξαρου ΒΑΣΙΛΕωΣ

מנושתר מן יאזתן ברי אלהא פאפכ מלכא
منوچتري من يزتان بري بگي پابكي ملكا
ΒΑΣΙΛΕωΝ ΑΡΙΑΝωΝ εκγενΟΥΣ ΘΕΩΝ ΥΙΟΥ ΘΕΟΥ ΠΑΠΑκου ΒΑΣΙΛΕΩΣ.

Image of the person of [Or]mazd-worshipper, divine ARTAKSHATR, *King of Kings* of Irán, of celestial origin from god, the son of divine PAPAK, King!

No. 1 a.

I. פתכר זניי ארהורמזד אלהא[2]
II. پتكري زني اوهرمزد يز..ي
III. ΤΟΥΤΟ ΤΟ ΠΡΟΣΩΠΟΝ ΔΙΟΣ ΘΕΟΥ.

Image of the person of ORMAZD, *God!*[3]

[1] The debased C = Σ, є = E, and ω = Ω, of the original inscription, have been replaced by the ordinary modern type forms of the several letters.

[2] The reading of Ormazd's name in the Chaldæo-Pehlvi is doubtful in the later copies (De Sacy, p. 27; Ker Porter, Pl. xxiii.; and Flandin, Vol. iv. Pl. 180); but it is obvious, as above given in Flower's reproduction, A.D. 1667 (Hyde, p. 547); and in Chardin's facsimile of 1674 (Pl. lxxiii. vol. ii.)

[3] Most of the linguistic details of this, or, perhaps, a less curt translation, have for long past been comparatively uncontested. The *Zend* I have not as yet had an opportunity of fairly or fully submitting to public criticism. The Mazd-Yaçna elements of the compound it has been the custom of late to recognise as "Ormazd-Worshipper," may perchance require re-examination when discovered to be associated with the full and direct definition of the name of ORMAZD, in apparent contrast to the abbreviated form, on one and the same stone. *Bagi*, with its palpable context of the Semitic *Alhá*, has from the first been accepted in its true purport, though doubts and difficulties remained in regard to the correct definition of the final *gi*, which are now, I imagine, fully disposed of. *Minu Chatri* (and מנו שתר) were freely interpreted by De Sacy with the aid of the Greek transcript, and all that more recent philology has been called upon to contribute has been the more exact determination of the roots and incidental formation of the compound in the now recognised منو or مينو, "Mundus superior," and the *Chitra* of such constant recurrence in the Cuneiform inscriptions and in the nominal combinations of the archaic Persian speech.

Inscription No. 2.

This inscription is engraved on an unfinished tablet, to the left hand, and immediately *outside* of the area of the bas-relief at Naksh-i-Rajab (Ker Porter, xxvii. No. 2; Flandin, 192 B), embodying one of the many representations of Ardeshir's receiving the cydaris from Ormazd: but there is nothing in the absolute relation of the two sculptures to show that the inscription in question was intended to refer to this particular group of the dynastic memorials graven on the surrounding rocks, though the probabilities are greatly in favour of such a supposition. Ker Porter does not seem to have been aware of the existence of this side compartment;[1] and although Morier[2] alludes to the single figure who is portrayed in the act of engrossing the identical record, he does not appear to have detected the inscription itself. It was left for M. Flandin[3] to repeat, in all innocence, a discovery which, in earlier times, had already been placed on record by Ouseley;[4] but to the former artist we are indebted for the only full copy known in Europe, which has evidently been most carefully traced on the spot and elaborately engraved in his work; but however meritorious as a studied and conscientious drawing, it is that and nothing more: had M. Flandin been but in the smallest degree acquainted with the crude forms of the eighteen letters of the alphabet employed in the text, the value of his labours would have been infinitely enhanced, possibly with far less patient toil to himself. As it is, this epigraph, the most full and perfect of the entire series, is disappointing in the extreme; and it is only by very bold guesses (such as no professed savant would adventure), that any recon-

[1] Ker Porter, i. 573. [2] Morier, "Persia, Armenia, etc." p. 138.

[3] Dans le coin à gauche, et en haut du rocher, en dehors du cadre où est sculpté le bas-relief, est une figure dont le buste seul a été exécuté. Peu visible par la manière dont elle est rendue, elle était en partie cachée par un arbrisseau qui avait pris racine dans une fissure du roc. En relevant les branches pendantes pour mieux voir cette figure, nous découvrîmes, sous leur feuillage, une inscription pehlvi très-bien conservée et qui n'avait pas moins de trente de une lignes presque complètes. Je crois pouvoir affirmer que cette inscription était complètement inconnue, car il n'en est fait mention par aucun voyageur. C'est donc une heureuse découverte, non-seulement pour l'étude de la langue pehlvi, mais encore pour l'intelligence de ce monument sur lequel elle jettera certainement un jour nouveau.—Text, vol. ii. p. 136.

[4] "Travels in Persia in 1810, 1811, 1812." vol. ii. pl. xlviii. No. 3.

struction of the purport of the original can be extracted from the distorted and disjointed characters in the French publication.

The inscription seems to have been originally executed in well-defined letters; but as far as M. Flandin's copy enables us to judge, no effort was made towards the separation or division of the words, nor are any of those very useful discriminative *final* i's to be detected in its lines. A large amount of independent synonyms may, nevertheless, be readily identified, though much concession has to be made for the uncertainty of the orthography of the period, and its manifest and startling contrast to the mode of spelling accepted in modern Persian: and in this consists almost the sole advantage of the inscription at this moment, in that even if one half of the terms now mechanically transcribed may be safely introduced into the meagre vocabulary of Sassanian Pehlvi hitherto authoritatively ascertained as opposed to the dubious and composite infiltrations of the ancient Pehlvi accepted in Bombay, some definite advance in this obscure study will be fairly established. I do not propose to enter into any analysis of this inscription, as I have but little faith in the trustworthiness of the text even in its now partially amended form. I may mention that the modern Pehlvi version here given adheres as scrupulously as possible to the engraved facsimile, while the Persian transcript is avowedly suggestive, and, as such, has been inserted more for the secondary purpose of aiding those who may need an introductory gloss upon the rarely-seen Pehlvi type, rather than for any authority that can be claimed for it. Indeed, in certain cases where the meanings of words were sufficiently obvious, I have departed from the limitation of mere reproduction, and modified the Persian correspondents in defiance of the imperfection of the Pehlvi original, in order to dispense with needless tests and references; but in many instances, where obscure passages recur in the Pehlvi, I have designedly changed the Persian equivalents assigned in the first instance, in the hope that one or the other of the optional modernised versions may hereafter lead to a correct determination of the value of the doubtful constructive elements of this, for the time being, obscure mediæval text.

The most curious question, however, relating to the inscription in its available form is, that in spite of its length and apparent completeness, as well as the free legibility of a portion of its contents, there are no means of determining, with absolute precision, the monarch in whose laudation it was composed. The natural impression suggested by the position in which the epigraph is placed points primarily to Ardeshîr Babekân, and several times in the text itself lend support to such a conclusion, the word كيتروم, from כתר, *a crown* (in line 27) more immediately connects the inscription with the bas-relief it may be supposed to explain; and, singular to say, it is not at all improbable that the missing name of Ardeshîr may after all be hidden amid the obscure cross strokes of the broken letters in the first line of the facsimile, the artistic imperfection of which, however, I have hesitated to correct in my Persian transcript, but which may fairly be converted, with very scant violence to probabilities, into هسني كرتير بگي ارتهشتر, a reconstruction that would sufficiently accord with the general tenor of the context, which concludes the current line with the conventional titular منوچيهر مين يزدان.

The unusual title of *Mîr Shahinshahi*, the latter a term specially affected by Ardeshîr, also connects the record with that monarch; as in like manner does the singular designation of ملكا زي شهپوهرين, "King of the King's sons," or what in modern days would be سلطان ساطين, a name or title indicative of royal origin, and so directly identified with the family intitulations, that Sapor retained the شهپوهر intact as his Imperial epithet.

Of the ordinary titles occurring in the course of the writing, some are highly instructive in regard to the comparative nomenclature of the period, such as هرپرست, "fire-worshipper" [priest] (2), ميرپست (28, 30, 31), ميري كرتير (23), ايهرپست (28) the Persian synonym[1] of the Greek *ἱεράρχης*, which latter term, however, when quoted from Western sources,

[1] The German philologists endeavour to identify the Greek *ἱερος* with *ishira* "robust." But a more simple association seems to present itself in the various words for *fire*, Pehlvi ־ר, Persian هير, Sanskrit इरिर.

was transmuted into the aspirated گیراك (Inscription V. 4). In addition to which may be cited پاتهشتري (24), पातृ, पत्, hodie پادشاه, etc.[1]

This inscription, even in its partially intelligible form, is also valuable as exhibiting so many of the essential characteristics of true Persian speech, in the multiplicity of the final i's, and in the dominance of the inevitable verb کردن, which even in this brief space crops up in all manner of moods and tenses.

[1] The following passages from the classic authors and other external sources, bearing upon the pompous intitulations affected by the successive ruling dynasties in Persia, are calculated to throw light upon the inquiry more immediately in question, as to the terms likely to be found in the original manifestors embodied in the court language and composed under official supervision, we have now to deal with.

ARSACES I.

"Certatimque summatum et vulgi sententiis concinentibus, astris (ut ipsi existimant) ritus sui consecratione permistus est omnium primus. Unde ad id tempus regis ejusdem gratis prætumidi, adpellari se patiuntur Solis fratres et Lunæ: utque Imperatoribus nostris Augusta nuncupatio amabilis est et optata; ita regibus Parthicis abjectis et ignobilibus antea, incrementa dignitatum felicibus Arsacis auspiciis accessere vel maxima. Quamobrem numinis eum vice venerantur et colunt, eousque propagatis honoribus, ut ad nostri memoriam non, nisi Arsacides is sit, quisquam in suscipiendo regno cunctis anteponatur: et in qualibet civili concertatione, quæ assiduæ apud eos eveniunt, velut sacrilegium quisque caveat, ne dextera sua Arsaciden arma gestantem feriat vel privatum."—Ammianus Marcellinus, xxiii. c. vi. § 4.

SHAPÚR II.

"Rex regum Sapor, particeps siderum, frater Solis et Lunæ, Constantio Cæsari fratri meo salutem plurimam dico."—Ammianus Marcellinus, xvii. c. 5, § 3.

"Agitatis itaque sub onere armorum vigiliis, resultabant altrinsecus exortis clamoribus colles: nostris virtutes Constantii Cæsaris extollentibus, ut domini rerum et mundi: Persis Saporem et Saansaan adpellantibus et Pyrosen, quod rex regibus imperans, et bellorum victor interpretatur."—Ammianus Marcellinus, xix. c. 2, § 11.

KHUSRÚ NAUSHÍRWÁN.

ἡ δὲ τοῦ Περσῶν βασιλέως γράμμασι μὲν ἐγγραφῇ Περσικοῖς, τῇ δὲ Ἑλληνίδι φωνῇ κατὰ ταῦτα δήπουθεν ἴσχυε τὰ ῥήματα· "θεῖος, ἀγαθός, εἰρηνοπάτριος, ἀρχαῖος Χοσρόης, βασιλεὺς βασιλέων, εὐτυχής, εὐσεβής, ἀγαθοποιός, ᾧτινι θεοὶ μεγάλην τύχην καὶ μεγάλην βασιλείαν δεδώκασι, γίγας γιγάντων, ὃς ἐκ θεῶν χαρακτηρίζεται, Ἰουστινιανῷ Καίσαρι, ἀδελφῷ ἡμετέρῳ."—Menander (Protector) de legationibus Romanorum ad Gentes, § 3.

BAHRÁM CHÚBÍN TO KHUSRÚ PARVÍZ.

Βαρὰμ φίλος τοῖς θεοῖς, νικητής, ἐπιφανής, τυράννων ἐχθρός, σατράπης μεγιστάνων, τῆς Περσικῆς ἄρχων δυνάμεως, ἔμφρων, ἡγεμονικός, δεισιδαίμων, ἀνεπανάλωτος, εὐγενής, εὐτυχής, εὐεπήβολος, αἰδέσιμος, οἰκονομικός, προνοητικός, πρᾷος, φιλάνθρωπος Χοσρόῃ τῷ παιδὶ Ὁρμίσδου.—Theophylactus Simocatta, iv. c. 7, § 18.

KHUSRÚ PARVÍZ.

Χοσρόης βασιλεὺς βασιλέων, δεσποζόντων δεσπότης, κύριος ἐθνῶν, εἰρηνάρχης, τοῖς ἀνθρώποις σωτήριος, ἐν θεοῖς μὲν ἄνθρωπος ἀγαθὸς καὶ αἰώνιος, ἐν δὲ τοῖς ἀνθρώποις θεὸς ἐπιφανέστατος, ὑπερένδοξος, νικητής, ἡλίῳ συνανατέλλων καὶ τῇ νυκτὶ χαριζόμενος ὄμματα, ἐκ προγόνων ἐπίσημος, βασιλεὺς μισοπόλεμος, χαριστικός, ὁ τοὺς Ἄσωνας μισθούμενος καὶ τὴν βασιλείαν Πέρσαις διαφυλάττων, Βαρὰμ στρατηγῷ Περσῶν, ἡμετέρῳ δὲ φίλῳ.—Theophylactus Simocatta, iv. c. 8.

TENTATIVE TRANSCRIPT OF INSCRIPTION No. II. IN MODERN PERSIAN.

1 هسني كرتير بگث رموت زي پون نزا . . . يهي . هزمنوچيهر من يزدان

2 يزيرهين هربرست ا . يهردزيكي يهي شين . زم پميرتي و زروني هراچ

3 ايزون پترهيت سيدهتاي و بزارو يزدان ارهكيتي هپاهزد ك . هيرن

4 از رادهي پاتكاسه كرتيهي هزماتون مفرينه ول رتلـ گدروس و چيتي

5 ودر شهري چهرني مهيهيت و ربي هنرتكتاي هدسون بزابتي . ريتيني پنچ

6 لسدر پروني ميزونكي هوي ركم پهرهيت اگيت مد . . يمت اهيتري يهوت‌ولد

7 اميرهي لوولي ول زيدان لرنيهت مهيت مومريا اهنهكس . . . . لي . . ييل شمس

8 و هيشتي و درسهري ول زك يزيست درانتاديهم و راتدي و هشمر دت

9 مهرهرت برسماه و هتاي و برامينداں زني ههبيم و يتمار

10 لشم زني مرزو و مهرهيت اديتت دم و دبير هميرهن امري و هرياشتر

11 يهشن هوي مرفرن نفشي چلودا مهاتيتري تهمي يهين

12 هوي مرمدم زني هيشتي و كرتكن [ك]بيرو شتري تيرتوسه

13 و ستاهيتري يهشن هوي مومنيا زي شوامكيه زي تنت

14 و پيت پورسات زك پون يزدان مشهتون سهي روبان راتي

15 و راستي ابر يهشن و مرمه زني يرنما شم هرتيتيري

16 ميكين پون بينديان كيريتوست ههترمياي مهرتسرتي

Inscription No. II.

1 [illegible]

2 [illegible]

3 [illegible]

4 [illegible]

5 [illegible]

6 [illegible]

7 [illegible]

8 [illegible]

9 [illegible]

10 [illegible]

11 [illegible]

12 [illegible]

13 [illegible]

14 [illegible]

15 [illegible]

16 [illegible]

17 من هرمني هرفرمان ارايوتزي ركمي ههنمي ايري دومن ايد

18 و هيشتي ايجي و درسهري ايتي يمني كريتري گدزراهور و هيشتي

19 و زرونت مرويچكري زكث ول درشهسرمي من رمن كريكرت هوي ومده

20 كريريت برسزيتنت ولي لزني تفترنديتريهي پنبرهي و ايمتيدب

21 يهمتونت ايش ولي استولدي روبا و پتاديهي من ميهمتونت

22 چيزونري كرتيري همتون ابم زني نامدي رهاچ. را و نفشتي ايد

23 ميري كرتير من كلي اولوني من شتردران ي مشهون بيراتري زكث

24 و مزونيرتي پاتهشتريهتي مردامم دبير و نفشي سمسراديهته

25 من مزتي پاتهشتري و ماتانيدتي بون هريمودت ايكث مزو پاستر

26 و دنا پاتهشتري ماتيدان اوريزتكي استاهورن امديهريتنت زكث

27 يدريتنت ايكاني زكث شتي و هوي مير شهنشهي و ملكان ملكا كيتروم

28 ميريت و ايهريت شمكرتي هريمي ايهرمك. ملكان ملكا و رنهاي ملكان

29 ملكا زي شهپوهرين كرتير زي اوهرمزدي ميريت شمكرتي هوي مشنهكن

30 ملكان . ول هلوه كرتير زي برزيزون روبان تپرايراوهرمزدي ميريت شمكرتي

31 هوي مسبشتي برهتكي دين . . . . كرتير سمشه

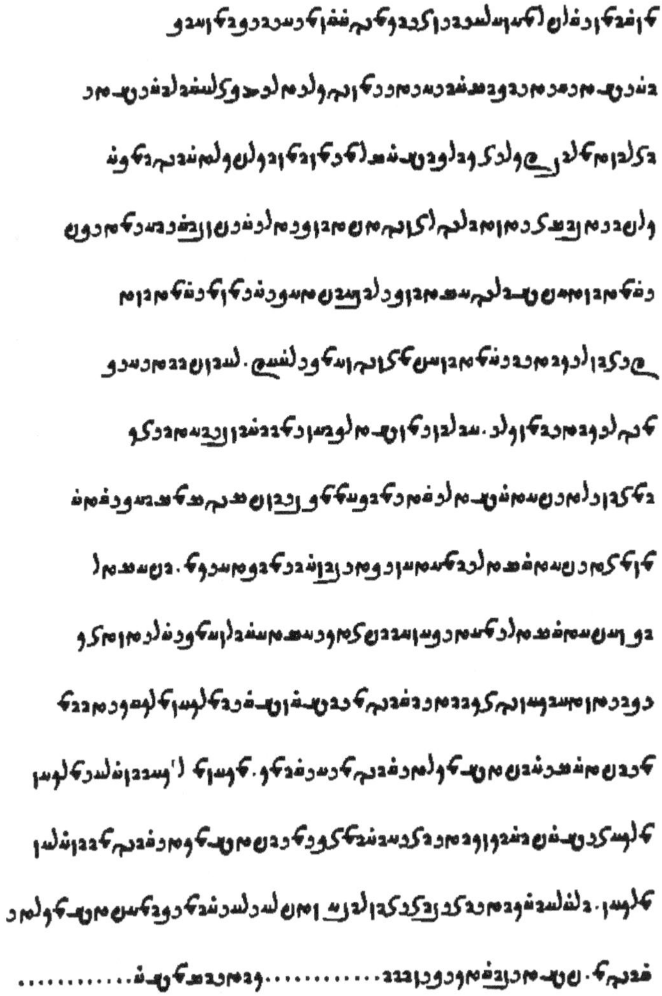

Inscription No. 3.—Pái Kúli Inscriptions—Sassanian.

Sir Henry Rawlinson has most disinterestedly entrusted me with his own private note-books containing his original sketches of the Pái Kúli Inscriptions, as well as with an earlier Cuneiform copy-book, in which I find Mr. Hector's independent tracings of the epigraphs on four of the slabs.

I have intentionally avoided submitting any of my tentative readings to Sir Henry, as not only has his time been of late fully occupied by more important duties, but I have been anxious that he should not be in the least degree compromised by any of my errors or imperfect interpretations derived from the fragmentary materials he has so amiably supplied me with.

1. The first inscription among Sir Henry Rawlinson's sectional copies is, perhaps, the most interesting of the whole series, giving, as it does, the name of Ardashir Bábekán, coupled with his title of King of Kings (ارتهشتر ملكان ملكا). The third line, like so much of the entire text, seems to continue his laudatory intitulation, زي ايران شتري, "of Irán King." The succeding line proceeds اتر كيدا شتري و فرمات, "Lord of the Fire Temple" (on whose terrace the inscription is engraved). The *Framáta* is here seen to retain its place in the official speech from the anterior date of the Cuneiform manifestoes of Darius,[1] while its modern counterpart perseveringly reaches our ears in the oft-cited *Firmáns* of the Porte. The conclusion of the record on this stone is obscure, and it is only by supposing extreme laxity of orthography in the original, and claiming, under such shelter, a momentary excuse for very hazardous suggestions, that the words may be rendered

[1] Persian version, x. 286, 310; Scythic, xv. 146; Persian (Oppert) J.A. 1852. p. 152. The grand Vizier of Persia, in later times, was called بزرگ فرماندار, in Armenian, *Vzourk-Hramanatar*. Journal Asiatique, 1866, p. 114.

Pái Kúlí Inscriptions.—Sassanian.

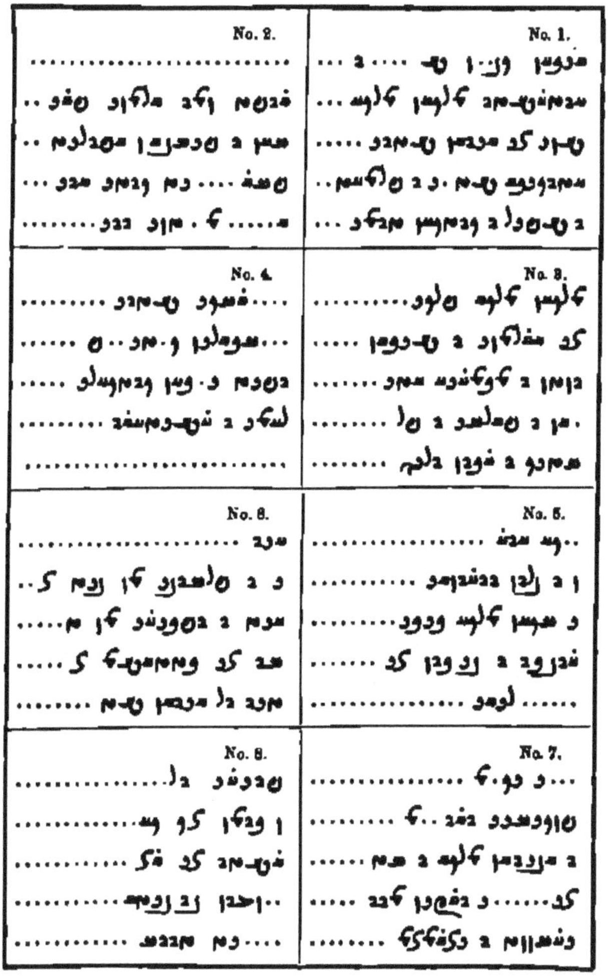

شفيل و كرتكان تومي, "Lord of Elephants,"[1] and Chief of Officials, otherwise "Head of the Executive."[2]

(2) The second lapidary sub-section opens with the words هربت نمر ارمني. The *Hirbad* (אירפת), Fire-Priest of the Scythian *Namri*,[3] a nomad tribe of ancient celebrity, possibly by this time permanently settled in close proximity to the kingdom of Armenia, with which their name is here associated.

(3) The third stone carries on the lines of a previous sentence in the title ملكان ملكا [يران ملكا – in Mr. Hector's copy], which is followed, perhaps connected with, the succeeding word نلكي, which admits of varying renderings from فَلَك, "heaven," نِلك, "a fire-worshipper" [بِلَك, "fire"], etc., according to the short vowels it may be necessary to supply, supposing always that even the three leading Pehlvi letters are assured in the modern Persian form in which they are here reproduced. The word occurs again in section 12, and in a questionably modified form in 21. The بارسي in line four answers to the province of Persia, and the ولي "Dominus," will be found to recur frequently in this and other inscriptions. (No. 14, etc.).

(4) The opening هسكي شتري in section 4, like so many imperfectly defined and, dubiously complete names, necessarily attracts attention without contributing in its isolated form the means of a positive identification; يزدان كرتكاري is fairly legible, and, with a continuous context, ought to present no difficulties. رامي, supposing it to be an undivided word, is

[1] (?) יקיר Chald. "beautiful."

[2] "*Tuma*," Tau'mâ (*Rawlinson*, J.R.A.S. x. pp. 101, 176, 196, etc.); Scythic, *tahma* (Norris, xv. 114, 134, etc.); "*Tahman*, fortis" (Fox Talbot, xix. 155); *Tâkhma* (Takhmuras; Haug, 194). تهم Oppert, J.A. xvii. 565. The superlative *Tuma* may have something in common with the term (Haug, 89), or possibly تومي may after all be merely an imperfect rendering of تخم, "race, seed, origin." *Cf.* Τεύχω, Τευχός, Τέκνον.

[3] Darius's Cuneiform Inscriptions, J.R.A.S. (Norris, xv. 180; Rawlinson, xv 236 and xix. p. 263); Oppert, J.A. 1857, p. 197.

readily recognizable, and associates itself with the technical رام, "rest," رامشتري, and other essentially Aryan terms.[1]

(5) No. 5 suggests but little worthy of remark beyond the combination of سكان ملكا. The name of Sakán is well defined, and the ي preceding the designation is carefully marked as a final.[2] The word بيدون is of frequent occurrence (v. 3, 6).

(6) The contents of No. 6 offer but little matter for safe speculation, with the exception of the concluding ايران شتر.

(7) No. 7 presents nothing remarkable beyond the ابيران ملكا which may be a mistake for انيران ملكا, owing to the mason, perchance employed indifferently on the duplicate epigraphs—having made use of a Chaldæo-Pehlvi א, a letter which is nearly identical in outline with the ordinary Sassanian B of these inscriptions.

(8) The commencement of the third line seems to retain the conclusion of the name of ارتبشتر. The title of بربيتان in line four also recurs frequently, and is readily identifiable with Anquetil's *Barbita* = "Salar en chef" (Z.A. ii. 486).

(9) The ninth tablet contains a title or, perhaps, a name of some interest, which may be read conjecturally, as هنگو or هرگويت; the designation occurs again in the sixth line, where it is preceded by the definite title of گيراك *Hierarch*. The هر probably stands for هير, "fire," as it is thus written in هربيت *Hirbad*; but the determination of the compound گويت is more open to question, unless it may be associated with the Sanskrit *Gupta* गुप्त from गुप् "to protect" (see also Nos. 17, 18, etc.). The word لبا which follows is possibly incomplete, but the obsolete Semitic לבי or לביא, "lion," so largely idealized and so consistently retained by the ancient kings in official seal devices and sculptured illustrations, and affectedly reproduced by the Sassanians in bas-reliefs and in titular composition as لبا كوشان, "lion slaying,"[3] might claim a leading dominance in this place, but it may be better to revert to the

[1] J.R.A.S. xiii. pp. 395, 399.
[2] "Saka," J.R.A.S., xii. 469; "Sacan," xv. 180.
[3] This term occurs on a beautiful gold coin of Hormusdas II. (303-310 A.D.).

term לִבָּא, "heart," لُبّ (from לְבַב, "to be fat"), which would more nearly accord with the general tenor of the inscription, and explain the frequent recurrence of the allied نفشي.

Among other words on this stone may be detected the important pronoun زك, "he," "who," "that," the original Persian Cuneiform 𐎹 (𐎹) *si*, "qui, que," also "quod, quia," which is associated with the Chaldee דִי, the relative pronoun and sign of the genitive.[1] The Hebrew זֶה, "this," the Arabic الّذي, "who," and ذَلِكَ, "that," have all to be considered in their bearing upon the word, as the duties the Pehlvi كو had to be answerable for were manifold. Anquetil was obliged to allow the term a very extended range of meanings in his single specimen page of Pehlvi translations of the Bun-dehesh (p. 341, vol. ii.); but in his vocabularies he rather limits it to "cela, celui-là," the modern Persian آن (pp. 496, 504).

The زي in these early Pehlvi readings seems to have been the contrasted form reserved for the sign of the genitive, which eventually settled itself into the ز of the Sháh Námah[2] and later Persian writings: while the زك, which was probably pronounced *zaka*, subsided into the present كه.

The شتري in line five is critically doubtful, as I have substituted, on the authority of the very indubitable form of

brought from Persia by Sir H. Rawlinson, and now in the British Museum. The following is a description of the piece: *Obverse*—King's bust, to the right; the head is covered with a lion's skin, after the classical precedent on the coins of Alexander the Great; this is again surmounted by flames of fire (?), at the back of which float the broad Sassanian fillets. Legend:

مزديسن بكي اوهرمزدي لبا كوشان ملكان ملكا

Reverse: The usual Fire Altar, to the right of which appears the figure of Ormazd (?) offering a chaplet to the king, whose form, together with the head-dress copied from the obverse, occupies the left of the altar. Legend:

مزديسن بكي اوهرمزدي لبا كوشان ملكان ملكا

Above the flame of the altar and below the circular legend the word ملكي is inserted.

[1] De Saulcy, J.A. 1855, p. 187.

[2] سپاهي زرومي و از پارسي ــ زبحرين و زكرد و ز قادسي. Macan. iii. 1422.

PAI KULI INSCRIPTIONS.—SASSANIAN.

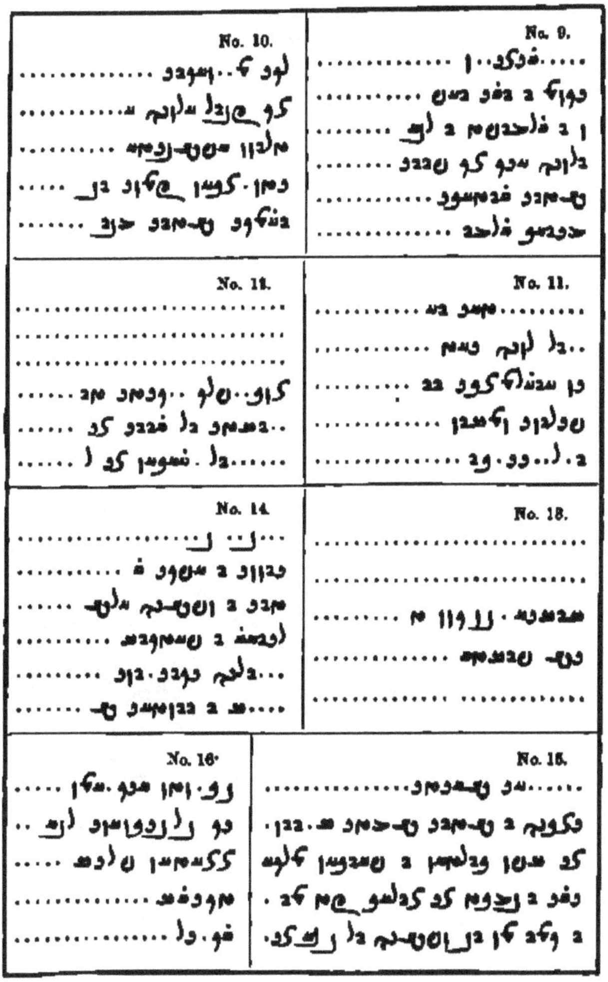

final given to the ي by Sir H. Rawlinson, an initial ش, in supercession of his apparent س.

The succeeding هرتا may, with equal propriety, be transliterated as هوتا, a form we should look for with much interest as a dialectic advance towards the ultimate orthography of خُدا, in spite of the incidental appearance of a later though, perhaps, more provincial variety of the title in shape of كدي on the coins of Firoz (A.D. 458-484). This is the *Khoda*, "Roi," of Anquetil (ii. 442, 515), and the conventional Pehlvi term for "king."[1]

(10) The tenth detached portion of the original mural record, among other words which need not be dwelt upon, concludes with وهمكي شتري كبر. It would be unwise to insist upon كبر, as, however appropriate, it appears in too unconnected and broken a form to be fairly relied upon.

(11) The eleventh stone is remarkable for the preservation of the name of Hormazd (اوهرمزدي=اوهلمزدي). The پيروني in

[1] M. Mohl (p. x. Preface, Shâh Nâmah) has suggested a very original but scarcely conclusive explanation of the disuse of this term in its proper and archaic meaning, by assuming that when the word خُدا came to be accepted by the followers of Muhammad in the sense of "God," that they were able to obliterate all ancient memories of the linguistic import of the designation, and to raise their *Allah* to the exclusively divine title, heretofore so simply affected in the ordinary acceptation of "king" by common mortals. It would, perhaps, be a more satisfactory way of explaining the difficulty, to infer that men of old, in the East, on attaining royalty, were given to advance a simultaneous claim to divine honours, and with this notion to assume the designations and attributes of their local gods; but as the world grew older, the words so employed reverted to their proper and normal linguistic import, which had been thus temporarily and conditionally misapplied; terms which, in the case in point, had already in a manner ceased to convey any exceptional mundane distinction. See a note on the subject of the Armenian god *H'aldis* in the *Numismatic Chronicle*, vol. vii. N.S. (1867) p. 161. Masudi tells us a good deal about the origin and use of the term; among other passages, in chap. xxiv. (vol. ii. p. 237, Paris edit.), he remarks—"Les rois perses, depuis l'origine des temps jusqu' à la naissance de l'islamisme, sont divisés en quatre dynasties. La première, qui s'étend de Keyomert à Aféridoun, est celle des *Khodahâns* (خداهان), mot qui a le sens de *rabb* (رَبّ) "maître," comme on dit *rabb-el-mâl* "maître d'un bien," *rabb-ed-dar*, "maître de maison." In the time of Khosrû Parvîz the State Seal for Khorasan still retained the title in خراسان خدا (p. 228). Aryan philologists propose to derive the word from خود آ, "self-coming" (خود آمدن), while the Sanskrit authorities suggest *Swadatta* स्व+दत्त, "self-given," or preferably *Swadhâ* स्व+धा, "self-generated." (Benfey).

line four may be another form of بيروني. which is a frequent adjective in the Sassanian inscriptions.

(12) No. 12, though much defaced, retains some indications of value in the possible restoration of line two, in the form of بريستي ول هوري. The word هور is not necessarily and exclusively "the Sun," but also applies to "fire, light," though the former interpretation is preferable in this place, as هر only occurs as the abbreviated form for *fire* in combination.

(13) The term پرستا again appears in No. 13, and is to be met with in various forms in the counterpart Chaldæo-Pehlvi version.

(14) The words انكي and پاتكرس, if we could but rely upon their correct isolation in the general and undivided continuity of the writing, would claim a passing notice, while the نفشي as a standard expression identifies itself with נפש, نَفْسُ, "life," "the vital spirit;" but the interest in this tablet centres in the conclusion, which, though greatly defective in the original, or its reproduction, seems to contain the word سوشنتاي. The *Soshyanto* of the Parsis were "the ancient prophets" of the Zoroastrian creed.[1] I must repeat that the divisions in the modern Pehlvi representation of Sir H. Rawlinson's *fac-simile* are purely arbitrary, and that I have no reserve whatever in altering or re-arranging the connection of the letters.

(15) No. 15 contributes a more ample legend than its fellows, and has the additional merit of being reported by its English transcribers as "very plain" in its writing; the words شاپتي, يزدي,[2] شتري are fairly legible towards the commencement; دولتان and پاردان,[3] followed by ملكا, appear in the third line; but the point of the highest interest in the whole inscription from first to last is the mention of the name

[1] Haug, Language of the Parsees, pp. 219, 196, 164. A far more serious and critical examination of the earlier chapters of the Zend Avesta, by Dr. Cajetanus Kossowicz, (Paris, 1865), gives *'Saoshyanç* as "Salvator."

[2] I am doubtful about this word, as the copy reads preferentially ي كدي The *Gs* and *Zs* are very difficult to distinguish in Sir H. Rawlinson's *fac-similes*.

[3] *Pertan* = Avestah-"pur" ou "Parole."—Anquetil, ii. pp. 448, 449.

of Zoroaster, with the appropriate introductory intitulation و بگدت زي زورادجست.[1] The detached passage concludes کمر من رب نفشي ول بيا زي.

(16) In the second line of No. 16 بريتال may be suggestively substituted for the بريدنان, which, however, I have faithfully represented in the Pehlvi, in strict accordance with Sir H. Rawlinson's copy.

(17) No. 17 is one of the most complete and most carefully traced of the whole series, but the facilities of interpretation are not, as yet, commensurate; the third line may be reproduced in modern Persian as شتردارسي بريتا ربا; line four admits of many optional conversions, but ربا , اهان بال is the best merely mechanical transcript; line five proceeds ملکا من وتن (وطن) نيکي هشن, and a very speculative restoration might define the contents of line six as شتري من درمن امير.

(18) No. 18 repeats the word هشن, or, as it may be preferably rendered, هروني, "Princely," and adds a third and very clear example of the هرگويت, preceded by the word کاروان. Though Mr. Hector's copy gives a totally different version of the contents of line three, which may be freely rendered کث ايران هري پش or هوي پور, while the هرگويت is transferred, in all its completeness, to line four.

(19) The nineteenth tablet, though very promising at first sight, seems to have been defective in the preservation of the definite forms of the letters. The opening شکري زمن may be suggested, as the first word occurs elsewhere. The conclusion of the last line gives the letters of يکشمون درهم; but Mr. Hector's transcript runs يکث شيکان شمون درهم.

(20) No. 20 presents us with the name of Tiridates, followed by the title of King, تيلدت ملکا. Tiridates was the early name of Sapor I. before he became prominent under the titular designation of "Son of the King," and the

[1] The Armenian version of the name is *Zradaschd*. E. Dulaurier, Journal Asiatique, 1852, p. 33. See also Haug, p. 252, for variants of the original designations.

PÂI KÛLÎ INSCRIPTIONS.—SASSANIAN.

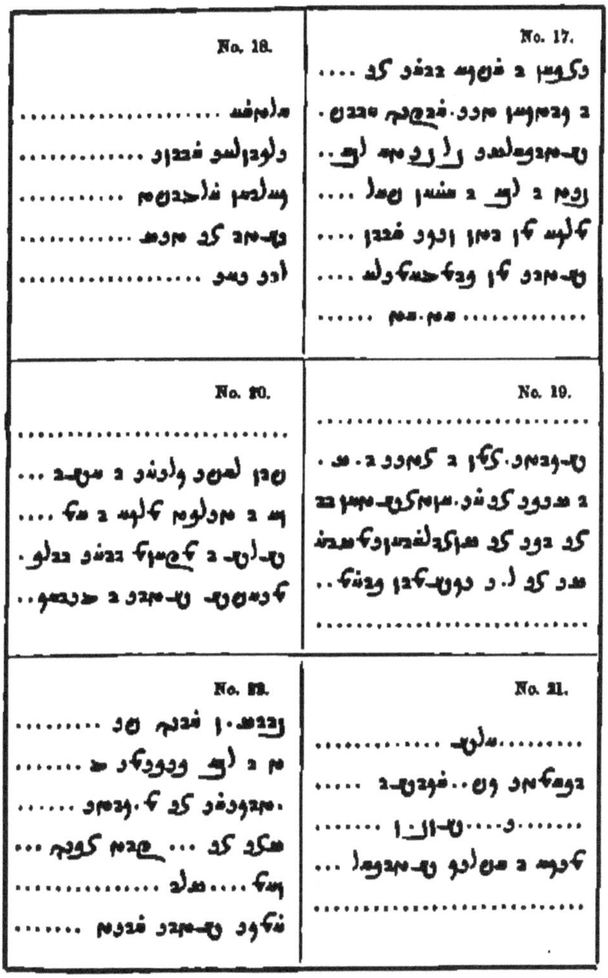

eventual associate in his father's sovereignty; though, in this instance, as his definitive identification and regal title appears in full in No. XXV. we are bound to conclude that the name of Tiridates here made use of applies to some other ruler or independent local Sovereign. In line three may be read, with every reserve, و مجانم شيئ ر ولد; but under a different arrangement of the words and a rejection of the dubious ش, the Pehlvi letters will equally correspond to مجان مروهي. The fourth line commences with a name optionally ميانش or ايش (مي), which is followed by the titles of شتري and گيراك, *ἱεράρχης*, *Hierarch*. Sir H. Rawlinson notices that there is a blank space at the bottom of the inscribed face of this stone, as if the last line of writing had formed a portion of the conclusion of the main inscription.

(21) The twenty-first tablet is considerably damaged and defaced; but the fourth line runs continuously ملكا و انليك شتردار.

(22) No. 22 is the last of the Sassanian series copied by Sir H. Rawlinson. In the first line may be seen the personal pronoun هوي (הוּא, Chald. הוה), Zend, *ava*, "he or she," the Cuneiform Persian *Hauva*, and the modern Persian اوي ,او ,وَي.[1] The second line gives the frequently-recurring روا, with a word which may be rendered ديديمي, a transliteration, however, that can scarcely be accepted in this place. The several terms تركيهي ,كرتي ,زدي, and نام may be tentatively modernized, and the concluding line may be restored under protest in regard to the original copy of the final يت as همكي شتري هريت.

[1] An apt illustration of the difficulty of expressing these and other gradational sounds in the imperfect Pehlvi alphabet is contributed by the anomalous state of the power of the literary definition in Kurdistán at the present day:—"Les Kurdes lettrés sont, en général, les gens qui ne savent qu' imparfaitement leur langue maternelle. Ils correspondent avec leurs autorités et entre eux-mêmes, soit en persan, soit en turc, soit en arabe. Si parfois ils se voient obligés d'écrire en kurde, ils le font à l'aide de l'alphabet persan. En effet, toutes les consonnes persanes sont identiques avec celles des kurdes, du moins pour ce qui concerne le dialecte de Soléimanié; mais celui-ci contient beaucoup de voyelles et de diphthongues qu'il serait impossible de reproduire au moyen de l'orthographe en usage chez les Persans. Comment, par exemple, figurer en persan les articulations *ae*, *ew*, *eo*, *dew*, *sew*, *dew*, *aow*, etc., qui se rencontrent si souvent et se suivent les unes les autres, sans l'intervention des consonnes, dans les mots kurdes?"—J. A. 1857, p. 302.

Pái Kúlí Inscriptions in Chaldæo-Pehlvi.

Sir H. Rawlinson's eye appears to have been less trained to the peculiarities of the Chaldæo-Pehlvi than to an appreciation of the outlines of the more simple letters of the fellow or Sassanian alphabet, so that while his transcripts in the latter character are, as it were, *written*, the former are elaborately but mechanically *copied*, and in some instances (Nos. 24, 27, 30, and 32), so great was the desire of accuracy, that the letters are traced in double lines, as is usual in exact engraving. The writing itself, as I have already pointed out (p. 11 *ante*) presents great sameness in the different alphabetical signs, and in many cases a very slight inflection constitutes the essential discriminative mark of the given letter. There are no obvious finals, and the words do not seem to have been separated, as is effected to a great extent in portions of the Hájíábád Inscription. Under these circumstances my conjectural restorations must necessarily partake, perchance even in a larger degree, of the imperfection of the materials at command: which of themselves appeared to promise and may, perchance, eventually afford a better text and a greater amount of information than their more voluminous counterparts in the Sassanian character.

In the ordinary course of the arrangement of the present article, under the conception of retaining in full prominence a systematic discrimination between the contrasted forms of the associate alphabets, I have reserved the closely-identical modern Hebrew type for the representation of the since-severed and now obsolete outlines of the Chaldæo-Pehlvi originals, while devoting the current Persian of our days to the embodiment of the Sassanian Pehlvi, from whose archaic elements it claims so much of direct descent. But on this occasion, where, in default of positive facsimiles, I have been obliged to elevate the Hebrew into a leading text, I resort to the less classic *Naskhi* type for my commentary, not only for the purpose of giving a second and possibly more suggestive identification of the true Persian original, in its now conventional alphabet, but also as affording a readier means of comparison with the *gloss* upon the more ample materials available in the less ephemeral Sassanian characters, which almost intuitively fell into the literal signs of that since amplified alphabet.

No. 23. The first of Sir H. Rawlinson's Chaldæo-Pehlvi Inscriptions, though carefully copied, is so imperfect in what remains of the original writing, that it would be useless to speculate upon any matter simply dependent on contexts. The word لبا, so frequent in the Sassanian series, occurs twice either in its full integrity or as a portion of other words, under the confessedly optional re-arrangement of the letters now presented, amid which it may be again remarked that no discriminative finals are to be detected.

No. 24 exhibits a more extended range of subjects for legitimate speculation. In the second line ز يازتن ربـ هشتر seems to be fairly assured in transliteration and simple in interpretation; the aspirated השתר, هشتر, the Sanskrit क्षत्र, from क्षि, "to rule," corresponds with the concurrent Sassanian شتر; while the פתיסא *Patisa* in line three recalls the ancient Cuneiform orthography. The preceding words وزونان و كرشمنين may, under very slight modifications, chance to carry new significance, as *Ionians* يونان (Greeks, etc.), and enemies دوشمنين, with the Chaldean plural termination and the long *a*, which is rejected in the modern orthography. The same remark may be applied to ايكن من لكما و هابتي in line four; and يازتن و هي كشاكني اسبتم, with much that is already intelligible awaits but little extraneous aid for satisfactory interpretation. In line six the oft-recurring بني is succeeded by יאזדן שמי *Ydztan Shamei*, "God of Heaven," which brings the whole tenor of the inscription back to Semitic regions; or, if a more distinctly Pehlvi rendering be sought in the شمي (the Pehlvi يون شمي دادار, "in the name of Almighty," the *Giver* of the Zoroastrian prayer), the context of the succeeding word may be improved into همكت شمت.

No. 23.

. . . . כרדא . . . .
. . . . רברבו . . . .
. . . . . פאסנכנ . . . .
. . . . לבא ו אזאת . . . .
. . . . המיסהותיד . . . .
. . . . לבא פרהש . . . .

No. 24.

. . . . זכאשו·חן . . . .
פושו · · ררכל ז יאזתן רב השתר
ו ותאן ו כרשכנין פתיסא . . .
איכ מן לכמא ו האפתי זכה ו
יאזתן והי כשאנגי אסבתמ . . .
פתי יאזתן שמיי המבה שמת .

No. 25.

. . . . כידהגיתיב . . . .
י אהיתית ו סכנדד לכ . . . . .
נה ו שתר ו שתאי מנו ר . . .
אן חשתר חסישתהותוי . . . .
וחלי ו הנת ו יהות הסנו . . . .
שהיפוהר מלכא כאושתר . . .

No. 26.

. . . ינשב . . . . . . יאזתא . . . .
ואכ יאכין ול נמינפשיי . . . . .
התאים ו ראבה שתרדדי . . .
ו פרמיתן ו מנ הדב פת א . .
. ל כמאל חיאת לגלי היתת .
וכ מנו פתגלאי תנ גאשת . . .

No. 27.

ראמ ו וישתאוהה . . . .
מיי אריאן השתר . . . .
מולנפתי יאזתן כאשת ו תר .
. זפרת ו אנכלין פואמר . . . .
. כתר ו כרתבני פתרהוינגי . .
. ראוית הרוא איבתג . . . . .

No. 28.

. . מלכא אריאן ו . . . .
הירתו רניפי ו . . . .
יתאימתן ו אתר·זכ . . . .
הג זמני · רב כחת . . . .
הות ו זפיבאתרש . . . .
זרוכאזודתרי . . . .

No. 25 exhibits in the second line the full constituent elements of the word "*Sakandar*," but the name seems out of place, and the isolation of the letters is altogether arbitrary. The יהוח - يهود in line five is of importance, as the designation, which can only apply to the Jews, will be met with hereafter in the Hájíábád Inscription; and, otherwise, there are many suggestive points in this text if we could but divide and determine the letters with anything like authority. The tablet concludes with the unmistakable name of Shápúr, conjoined with the adjunct of "king" in their proper Semitic forms of שהיפוחר מלכא شهپوهر ملكا.

No. 26. After a detached or incomplete word of no present importance, the first line terminates with the letters يازتا, which are dubiously suggestive of *Avesta*. The اكي اكين of line two is followed by the Arabic ال (Pehlvi ول), and the name of نمي (perhaps نمر) is succeeded by the oft-recurring نقشي. Line three seems to read هٔخايم وراپ هشترد‌ري (Inscrip. No. VI. lines seven and twelve); line four proceeds وفرميتن ومن هرب يت—, the latter combination is curious if we may rely upon the transliteration. كمال حياة is followed in line four by the لكلي, which there will be further occasion to notice in the Hájíábád Inscriptions. يتكلي تن كاشت concludes this section, though I must confess that I have but little confidence in the existing data or the result now obtained from them.

The transcription of the first line of No. 27 may be optionally varied from the Hebrew text to رام و تشتاوه هـ as the letters are very imperfectly preserved. اريان هشتر is clear in line two. مزلن or ميلن يتي followed by يازتن كاشت may be suggested as a tentative reading of line three; and, under even more reserve, زترت و انكلين پوامر for the fourth line. راويت هريزا ايهن may be received for the moment as a possible reproduction of line five.

The 28th tablet commences with ملكا اريان, "King of Irán." In the second line may be doubtfully traced a variation of the name هیرکو followed by some damaged letters forming the word دنیبي or رلیبي. Line three is likewise defective in the outlines of the letters, which, however, may be tentatively rendered یتایمون, و اتر-زکث or ایر-زکث. Line four runs مهن زمني رب کوزت—. Line five, under a mere servile reproduction of the original copy, may be transcribed سهوت و زتیباترش; but the second word is freely convertible into یپزکا or other possible variants. The sixth line contains the letters زدو کازو رتري.

29. The legible portions of this section comprise letters answering severally to هشتر و همکث هشترایشا. Line four, لن پت و پوشت [پرشتو] وشمي مي. Line five, پنر پلیکث ملکا و مکورن ملکا. Line six, و باتیز ودکتشن هوتوپ و.

No. 30 commences هشتر استبکث. Line two continues from a preceding tablet پیتي هشتر هرتلین. Line three, to judge from the copy, must be much damaged, پتي at the beginning and ایکث at the end are all that can be relied upon. The letters decipherable in line four contribute the following possible combination: کبوي دودن پرشکرت.—The سریه کرتیر in line five, if correct, is exceptional, as the ever-recurring verb کردن of the Sassanian system has not hitherto been met with in this Chaldæo-Pehlvi transcript. The سپول in line six may equally well be converted into ستول, پتول, or other new combinations; for among the originally fully-contrasted forms of the ancient letters I can extend no certain faith to Sir H. Rawlinson's copies of the פ and the ת, as discriminated from one another: and worse still, the ס, which, at the time his copies were made, was unknown, or rather unproven,—may so easily be taken for either of the approximated outlines of the first-named more common letters, that the natural difficulties of a right interpretation of the damaged writings of Pái Kúlí are almost hopelessly enhanced! The apparently isolated words which stand at the foot of this tablet seems to afford a second example of a derivation of the verb کردن in the form of کرثي.

In No. 31 the previous reading of فرميتن in No. 26 is fully confirmed by its definite repetition in this place. Line two suggests many uncertain details, though the best version seems to be ورديو اياله اميوت ركنت ومن ـه. But the interest of this tablet centres in line three, where, if we could rely upon our standard text, we might transcribe freely the words و باترو ماكيرش اكيالت و بترو كرتكني; a variant of the اكيالت has been met with before in No. xxvi., but the ماكيوش, if it could be assured, would throw additional light upon this apparently religious manifesto of the Zoroastrian creed. The بتيسه (possibly the بتيسا of No. xxiv.) commences line four, followed by هشتر كريت و يايكلن كنهيت. The هوبتي of the printed text in line five may require correction into هريتي. The اكايمود at the end of the line is a word to be compared and commented on hereafter. يازتن كربي و هشتر complete all that remains of the last line.

The 32nd and last tablet is the most curious of the whole broken series, and in the seeming completeness within itself, as judged by its remaining fragments, must have either constituted a portion of a summary or recapitulation apart from the rest of the inscription, otherwise any preconceived idea of the absolute continuity of the text from stone to stone in the ordinary line of writing must be altogether at fault. Though it is by no means improbable that the record of the original manifesto of Ardeshir was finished after the accession of Sapor, even if it was not supplemented by him with independent tablets devoted to his own glorification. Such an inference would accord well with the frequent appearance of Sapor's name, as associated with the full honors of royalty, in certain passages whose consecutive order it is, at present, impossible to determine. The five letters still extant in the first line resolve themselves almost naturally into the Aryan ناگرا (नगर), but the long vowels tend to cast a doubt about the identity of the word. After some obscurities, line two presents us with the word سورين, which, adverting to the sub-

No. 30.	No. 29.
השתר אסתנבב	מותאיב . . . .
פיתי השתר הרתלין	כדכתר . . . .
פתי ו ח · ח · היתת איב	השתר ו הכב השתר אישא ·
כהויירוהנ פרשכרת	לנפת ו פושת ו שמיי מיי . . .
סריתכרתי רש	פנרפלוכ מלכא ו מבורן מלכא
ספולשיה · · · ל · תכנ	ו כאתי זורכתשן הותיי ו . . .
. . . . כריי	. . פאכר . . . . . תדד . . . . .

No. 32.	No. 31.
. . . . נאנרא . .	פרמיתן ו אכח . . . .
. . ו סורין ונמתיתאתר	הומנרכנכ אמות איאלה ו רהיו . . . . . .
פארס ו כרנת ותן ו אסור	ופאתרו כרתבני פתרה ו אכיאב מאגיוש
ארמינר ו אריאן השתר	פתיסה ו כנהית ו יאיכלן חשתר כרית . .
. . אתהשתרי מלכא ו כ	הופתי השתר הות ו . . . אבאימור . . .
מנו . . . . . . אמארלישתפ	אותן כריי ו השתר . . . .

sequent associations, may possibly stand for the country of Syria, but which I prefer to consider as the ancient, much-esteemed title of *Surena*, a name the Romans learned to know but too well in the course of their Persian wars.[1] The country of پارس *Persia* seems clear enough; کرگست وتن (وطن) presents a

[1] Plutarch in Crassus; Strabo, xvi. c. i. § 24; Ammian. Marcell. xxiv. c. ii. § 4, c. iv. § 12; Zosimus, iii. c. xv.; Mos. Khor. i. 313; J.A. 1866, p. 130. The title was possibly derived from سَر, "King" (سَرين) There is a term having something of the like import in Modern Persian in سورِستار, "Regis Minister" (Vullers).

difficulty, but اسور *Assyria* can scarcely fail to represent that even then renowned kingdom. ارمينر, in line four, may reasonably be corrected into *Armini*, especially in its direct conjunction with اريان هشتر. The name of ارتهشتري is confessedly a restoration out of the very imperfect tracing of the original pencil copy, but the letters אתחשתר are sufficiently assured to justify the insertion of the missing ר after the initial, and the needful termination before מלכא. The concluding line is nearly illegible.

Sir H. Rawlinson has favoured me with the subjoined Note on the locality and surroundings of Pái-Kúli, which unfortunately reached me after the preceding pages had been set up in type.

These ruins which I first heard of in 1835 whilst employed in the neighbouring district of Zohab (see Journal of the Royal Geograph. Soc., vol. ix. p. 30), I had an opportunity of examining in some detail during a two days' visit which I paid them in 1844, in company with Mr. Alexander Hector, on a return trip from Sulimanieh to Baghdad. They are situated at the South-Eastern extremity of the rocky ridge of Seghermeh, at the distance of about four miles from the right bank of the river Shirwán or Diyáleh, and just beyond an easy pass which crosses the shoulder of the hill from the Karadagh valley. The hill which intervenes between the ruins and the river, and which is a lower and less rugged continuation of the Seghermeh range, is named Gúlán. The district on the river is called Bani-Khilán, and is well known from the ford of that name by which the river is crossed on the high road from Zohab to Sulimanieh. The exact position of the ruins is in latitude 35° 7′ 16″, and longitude 45° 34′ 35″. With these indications any traveller may succeed in finding the locality, but to enable him to inspect the ruins at his leisure it will be indispensable that he should be attended with a suitable escort, as the districts along the river, being a sort of debatable ground between the Persian and Turkish empires, are overrun with marauding Kurds who pay no respect to either Prince or Pasha.

The ruins, which are called indifferently *Pái-Kúli* ("the

foot of the pass"), and *But-Khaneh* ("the idol temple"), crown the summit of a shoulder which runs out from the range towards the East and thus presents a sloping declivity circling round from N.E. to S.E. It is difficult to determine the design of the original edifice, so completely has it been ruined, but it may be conjectured to have been a quadrangular construction, about one hundred feet square, formed of rubble and brick and faced with large blocks of grey stone of which the exterior surface was smoothened; and probably the building itself was crowned with a cupola. At present indiscriminate heaps of brick and mortar, rubble and stone, cover the entire summit of the hill, and nowhere is any portion of the wall in its original state to be recognized. Scattered along the brow, however, and at different points on all three sides of the steep slope, which extends perhaps 150 yards from the ruins to the plain below, are to be seen at least 100 blocks of hewn stone, the débris apparently of the building above; and as a considerable number—perhaps half—of these blocks are engraved on their smoothened face with writing, and the inscribed blocks would all seem to have fallen from the Eastern wall of the building, I conceive that it was on that face only, fronting the rising sun, that the commemorative record was placed. This record, like most of the other memorials of the early Sassanians, was engraved in two different characters and languages, which used to be called Parthian and Sassanian, but which it is now proposed to distinguish as Chaldæo-Pehlevi and Persian-Pehlevi. I copied the inscriptions on thirty-two blocks of stone, ten of these inscriptions being in Chaldæo-Pehlevi and twenty-two in Persian-Pehlevi; and these were all the fragments of writing which were exposed and which were tolerably legible; but there are, I doubt not, an equal number of fragments still to be recovered by any traveller who has the means and the leisure to turn over the many blocks lying with their face downwards, and also to disinter those which are now half imbedded in the soil, or covered over with the rubbish, on the summit of the hill. Amongst this rubbish I further observed one slab about four feet square, rudely sculptured with the head and shoulders of a Sassanian king, the figure being intended in all probability for Ardeshir Babegan; and it is very possible other similar slabs would be found if the ruins were thoroughly examined. I always, indeed, cherished the idea of being able, on the occasion of some future visit, to take an exact paper-cast of the inscribed surface of every block throughout the ruins, by which means I might succeed in reconstructing the work, after the manner of a child's puzzle; and I am still of opinion that this reconstruction might be partially, if not completely, effected,—notwithstanding that the edges of the blocks are in many cases chipped and worn;—since it would be assisted, not only by the coincidence of the lines of writing, but by the identifications of the different words and phrases as the general tenour of the inscriptions became gradually intelligible.

It only remains that I should say a word as to the purport of the original building. In popular tradition the place is known as the *But-khaneh* (or "idol-house"), probably from the figure of Ardeshir, which is still the prominent feature of the ruins; but I found that the educated Kurds—and there are many such at Sulimanieh—considered Páï-Kúlí to be the site of a Fire-Temple of the Magi; and such I believe to be a true explanation of this really interesting spot, although I have never met with a notice of the locality among the many copious descriptions of Sassanian antiquities that are found in the early Arabic Historians and Travellers, and although the inaccessible position of the ruins and the present desolate and inhospitable character of the surrounding country are singularly inappropriate to a great scene of popular pilgrimage. In all probability, however, the country has very much altered in appearance since the Sassanian period. At present there are no permanent villages or fixed inhabitants between the Turkish frontier at Khannikín and Sulimanieh, but along the course of the Diyáleh, throughout this interval of space, are to be seen on both banks numerous traces of ancient populousness and prosperity. On the Persian side of the river, for instance, the ruins of Sheikhán, of Hurín, and Herabel have been already described by me (see Geograph.

Journal, vol. ix. p. 30), while in following the Páï-Kúlí route from Sulimanieh to Khannikín, I now found a series of ancient remains which convinced me that the old road conducting from Ctesiphon to the Atropatenian Ecbatana must have followed this line. The road in question is mentioned by many of the early Arab geographers (by Ibn Khurdadbeh, for instance, and by Mosáer, as quoted by Yacút in the Mo'ejem-el-Baldán); it left the great Persian road at Ḳaṣr-i-Shirín, and proceeded north to Dér Kán, now called Housh Kerek, where there are some extensive and very remarkable Sassanian ruins; it crossed the Diyáleh at Binkudra, a corruption of the old Syriac title of Ba-Nihudra, and led from thence to Shirwáneh, a place which has given its name to the river and where there is a magnificent artificial mound, that would be well worth excavating. Further on there are the remains of an extensive city near the river, now called Shar-i-Verán ("the ruined city"), but which I cannot identify in ancient geography. An easy stage conducts from Shar-i-Verán to Páï-Kúlí, and from that point the old road crossed the Goura Kileh ("Gueber's fort") range, which is a S.E. prolongation of the Karadagh hills, direct to Yasín Teppeh, the ancient Shahrizúr, leaving the modern town of Sulimanieh at least fifteen miles to the left hand. This route was of great importance under the Sassanians. An ancient custom, dating probably from the time of Ardeshir, required that each king should on his accession proceed from Ctesiphon along this road to be crowned in the Fire-Temple of Azerakhsh at Shíz; and in connection with such a line of pilgrimage Shahrizúr itself acquired such celebrity that it was popularly named *Ním-ráh*, or "the half-way house," the distances respectively from Ctesiphon to Shahrizúr by the Páï-Kúlí route, and from Shahrizúr to Shíz (or Takht-i-Sulimán), being about 185 miles, as explained by me in my examination of the march of Heraclius on Ganzaca in the tenth volume of the Geographical Journal, p. 101. I think it very probable, then, that the Fire-Temple at Páï-Kúlí was instituted in connection with this route from Ctesiphon to Ganzaca, and that the legend, the fragments of which are here published, may contain some allusion to the royal progresses.

H. C. RAWLINSON.

INSCRIPTION No. 4.

The bas-relief at Naksh-i-Rajab,[1] which the subjoined inscription is intended to illustrate, consists of a group representing Sapor heading a procession on horseback, while around and behind him are ranged the nobles of his court with his guards on foot. The face and head-dress of the monarch have been intentionally damaged, but the slope of the coronet of the latter can be traced in outline, and seems to accord with the low mural crown depicted in other sculptures and ordinarily in use upon his coins; this is surmounted by the customary globe of fire or ether; side masses of bushy curls, with the national fillets fluttering lightly at the back, complete the details the iconoclast has suffered to remain.

One of the peculiarities of Sapor's costume as contrasted with the more simple garments of his father, which hang heavily and formally over his limbs,[2] is that his vestments seem to be composed of silk or linen of the finest texture, and fall wavily and lightly in their folds, with their loose ends floating freely in the air. The inscription, as in an earlier example (No. 1), is engraved as far as space permitted on the shoulder of the charger. The immediate attendants wear various forms of the Parthian helmet,[3] with distinguishing devices on the right side of the casque, the subordinate guards who fill in the rear of the design wear uniform but unadorned helmets of the Parthian pattern, and stand with their hands crossed over the hilts of the long straight sword in use at the period.

[1] Niebuhr, ii. pl. xxxii. p. 126; Ker Porter, pl. xxviii; Flandin, bas-relief A, pl. 189, and enlarged engraving, pl. 191; De Sacy, p. 31; Ouseley, Travels, pl. lv.; Rich. Babylon, pl. xii.; Ker Porter, vol. i. pl. 28; Flandin, vol. iv. p. 573, pl. 190.

[2] See Ardeshir in pl. xxiii. and xxvii. fig. 2, Ker Porter; and 182 and 192 Flandin.

[3] "Their helmets of Margian steel polished to the greatest perfection." Plutarch in Crassus. Am. Marc. xxiv. c. 4, § 5.—There is a specimen of one of these caps in the British Museum; it is a head-piece of considerable merit, light, well-balanced, with a good slope from the sides towards the crested ridge at the apex, and anything but after the design of the apparently top-heavy Parthian caps, the profile system of representation reduced those helmets to in rock sculpture and coin devices.

INSCRIPTION No. 4.—SHÁHPÚR I. A.D. 240–273, at Naksh-i-Rajab.

I. פתכר זניי מזדיין אלהא שהיפוהר מלכין מלכא אריאן ו

II. پتكري زني مزديسن بگي شهپوهري ملكان ملكا ايران و

III. ΤΟ ΠρΟΣΩΠΟΝ ΤΟΥΤΟ ΜΑΣΔαΣΝΟΥ ΘΕΟΥ ΣΑΠωΡΟΥ ΒΑΣΙΛΕΩΣ

אנאריאן מנושהר מן יאותן ברי מזדיין אלהא ארתחשתר מלכין

انيران منوچتري من يزتان بري مزديسن بگي ارتهشتر ملكان

ΒΑΣΙΛΕΩΝ ΑΡΙαΝΩΝ ΚΑΙ ΑΝΑΡΙΑΝΩΝ ΕΚ ΓεΝΟΥΣ Θεων υἱου ΜΑΣΔαΣΝΟΥ

מלכא אריאן מנושהר מן יאותן בריי אלהא פאפך מלכא

ملكا ايران منوچتري من يزتان نبي بگي پابكي ملكا

ΘεΟΥ ΑΡΤΑΞΑΡΟΥ Βασιλεως ΒΑΣΙΛΕΩΝ ΑΡΙΑΝΩΝ ΕΚ γεΝΟΥς θεων ΕΚΓΟΝΟΥ ΘΕΟΥ ΠΑΠΑΚΟΥ ΒΑΣΙΛΕΩΣ.

Image of the person of [Or]mazd-worshipper, divine SHAHPÚHR, *King of Kings* of Irán and Anírán, of celestial origin from God, the son of [Or]mazd-worshipper, divine ARTAKHSHATR, *King of Kings* of Irán, of celestial origin from God, the son of divine PAPAK, *King!*

INSCRIPTION No. 5.

The text of Inscription No. 5, in its full development, originally formed the illustrative commentary on one[1] of the best executed of the many rock sculptures[2] to be found in various

[1] Ker Porter, pl. xxl.; Flandin, pl. 185.

[2] This calamitous incident in the annals of the Roman Empire is treated under various modified details in the different sculptures devoted to its representation. At Dárábgird (plates 31 and 33, Flandin), Sapor places his left hand on the head of Cyriades, as if in commendation, or confirmation of the position he was about to bestow upon him, in supersession of the kneeling Valerian. Sapor's helmet is, in this instance, similar to the skull-cap ordinarily appropriated to his father, but the tied point of the beard continues to mark his special identity.

In plate 48 of Flandin (bas-relief B, at Shâhpûr), we have a single kneeling figure before the horse of the conqueror without the usual incidental accompaniments. In plate 49, bas-relief A, also sculptured at Shâhpûr, the positions of the parties are greatly changed; and if we may judge by the seemingly elaborate drawings, the younger man is now kneeling, possibly awaiting investiture, while Sapor places his right hand on the arm of Valerian, who is clearly in fetters, as if in the act of exhibiting him to the assembled troops. Sapor's crown in this bas-relief follows the usual mural pattern. A novelty is to be noticed in this composition in the introduction of a winged figure descending from the sky and presenting to Sapor a second diadem, which floats in unbound and open folds. See also Morier's plate xiii. p. 91, Persia, Armenia, etc. London, 1812.

Plate 53 is indistinct in the definition of the persons forming the general group, but Valerian is seen kneeling with hands outstretched in the ordinary attitude, while a standing figure behind him, in the garb of a Roman, presents a circlet to Sapor. The outline of the figure standing by the side of Sapor's charger

parts of Persia, devoted to the commemoration of Sapor's successful capture of the Emperor Valerian in 260 A.D. The general arrangement of Sapor's dress in this instance is similar

is imperfect, but from the size it would seem to be designed to represent a youth. The angel with the Sassanian bandeau appears above, and in the side compartments are figured a Roman biga, an elephant, a horse, etc.

I am unable to recognise in plate 51, bas-relief D (Morier, pl. xi.) at Shâhpûr, any association with Sapor's triumph over Valerian, but understand the general design to refer to some other boasted success of the Persian monarch, perchance over the Syrian king Sitarûn (Mas'udi, cap. lxxviii.) or possibly over Odenathus himself, who, under western testimony, is affirmed, on the other hand, to have gained advantages over Sapor in the war undertaken to avenge the humiliation of the Romans. Sapor's portrait in this sculpture is more artistic in its treatment than usual; and if Flandin's copy, here reproduced, be a true rendering of the original we may fairly admit the traditional perfection of that monarch's form and features.

HEAD OF SAPOR I.
From a Bas-relief at Shâhpûr.

The head dress is changed from the ordinary mural crown into a close-fitting cap, from the sides of which rise eagles' wings, and the whole is surmounted by the conventional globe. This style of head-gear is used by Sapor in the bas-relief Ker Porter, xxiv.; Flandin, plates 187, 188; but it does not appear on the coins of the dynasty till the reign of Varahran II. (279–296), who employs it throughout. Among the other head-dresses of Sapor may be noticed a sort of Parthian cap or helmet coming to the front in the head and beak of an eagle. (*Numismatic Chronicle*, xv. p. 180, fig. 3).

to that already adverted to under the notice of No. 4 bas-relief, but the face and head-dress are here admirably preserved; the former exhibits much of the manly beauty for which Sapor was so famed,[1] with a delicate though well-formed moustache, closely-curled or partially-grown whiskers, passing into a well-trained beard, which is retained in a quaint tie below the chin, so as to create a small prolonged imperial below the ring or binding which checked its natural flow, a fashion which, even in Sapor's own time and afterwards, merged into a jewelled drop, constituting a terminal completion of the beard itself, and whose exaggerated dimensions formed so marked a peculiarity in the medallic portraiture of later sovereigns! Sapor has the usual bushy side-curls, and still adheres to the mural crown surmounted by the conventional globe,—the Sassanian fillets float freely at the back, and similar small fillets or barred ribbons are attached to his sword hilt, his ankles, and even to his horse's head and tail. Valerian is fitly represented in the Roman costume, with the laurel chaplet on his brow, kneeling in front of Sapor's charger, with both hands outstretched, in the obvious attitude of supplication; a young man, also in Roman garb, wearing an identical chaplet, and who is supposed to be intended for Cyriades, stands by his side and receives from the hand of Sapor the circlet and wavy bands, which other sculptures indicate to be the accepted insignia of royalty.

The inscription itself, which fills in the space behind Sapor's horse, was partially copied by Niebuhr,[2] and a few lines were sketched but not published by Ker Porter.[3] M. Flandin's[4] transcript is a most marked advance upon the early tracings of Niebuhr in the amplitude of the text, though only questionably improving upon the legibility of the selected sections contributed by his predecessor. We have most indubitable evidence in the portions now intelligible that the inscription emanated

[1] Mas'udi—*French edition*, ii. p. 160, iv. p. 83; Mirkhond, in De Sacy, pp. 285-7.
[2] Voyage en Arabie. C. Niebuhr. Amsterdam, 1780. Vol. ii. pl. xxxiv. p. 129.
[3] Ker Porter, i. 641.
[4] Flandin, vol. i. pl. 181, p. 641.

from Sapor (line 1, 2, 6, etc.), whose name and title of Malkán Malká there can be no misreading, and equally is it clear that the great Hierarch of Hierarchs, whose designation is so often repeated, refers to the unhappy Roman "Pontifex Maximus," Valerian himself.[1] It will be seen that none of the bas-reliefs, commemorating the capture of Valerian, give any countenance to the loose accusation of the Western writers regarding the severity of the treatment or wanton humiliation of the Roman Emperor on the part of Sapor. On one occasion only, in the entire series of sculptures, is Valerian represented in chains, and the anklets, in this case, may well be taken to be merely figurative. The few Persian authors, indeed, who notice this but little appreciated episode in the history of their own country, relate that Sapor wisely took advantage of the engineering skill of his captive, and employed him, together with free artizans obtained from Rome, in the construction of the celebrated irrigation dam, and in the general embellishment of the new city of Shuster. Tabari, it is true, reports that after completion of these works, Sapor marked and disfigured his prisoner, but the statement bears but little semblance of truth, and the Sháh Námah, in its version of the details, makes no allusion to any such barbarity. It is singular that in no one instance is there to be found any sign of the strictly western form of the name of Valerian, the Persian word *shatri*, in two several instances, precedes the other designations applicable to the dignity he was supposed to hold; and on the second occasion (line 11), this local title is connected with an outlying final or possibly directly initial *ul*, which, under the free licence of interpretation, the crude orthography of the associate texts fully invites, may be held susceptible of conversion into *Val shatri*,[2] which perchance, may have conveyed to the *indigènes*

[1] Eutropius, ix. c. 6; Zosimus, I. c. 36; Agathias, iv. 23; Trebellius Pollio in Hist. Aug. VI. vol. ii. p. 179; Aurelianus Victor de Cæsaribus, xxxii., and Epitome, xxxii.; Lactantius, "de mortibus persecutorum," c. v.; Eusebius, ii. 301; Zonaras Ann. xii. 23; (U.C. 1010); Abulfarage, p. 81; Gibbon, I. p. 459; Clinton, Fasti Romani, I. 284. Coins of Valerian cease with A.D. 260-1. His name, however, appears in one law of A.D. 262, and in a second of 265. Eckhel, vol. vii. 387.

[2] *Val* was a favourite name in these lands—as *Val* Arsaces, *Val*, King of Edessa

the nearest approximate sound of the Grecized adaptation of the original [ΟΥΑΛΕΡΙΑΝΟΣ].

The introduction of the name of AUHARMAZDI with the suffix *Malkán Malká* is strange in the extreme, if the worldly titles are supposed to be applied to the *Divinity*; but it might be better in the present state of our knowledge, and the defective context of this inscription, to limit the attribution of the designation to the Hormuzdas, the son of Sapor, who eventually succeeded to his father's throne, notwithstanding that the titular honors here conceded equal those of the reigning monarch.

There is very much else in this inscription calculated to invite comment under the linguistic and philological aspects, with so many words that may be reduced into their simplest modern forms by, so to say, the merest turn of the pen: but my object, in transliterating these primarily conscientious though necessarily deceptive reproductions of a nearly obliterated lapidary text, is accomplished in affording more ready means of comparison to future copyists, and determining a certain number of words for the illustration and confirmation of my leading text.

With regard to the restored modern Pehlvi version now printed, I may remark that I have adhered as closely as possible to the very letters given in the servile engravings from which it has been drawn.

In the case of the ordinary Persian transcript, I have allowed myself occasional latitude in suggestive modifications; but, as a general rule, I have merely transcribed the old character into its modern form, leaving the multifarious optional correspondents of the ancient letters to be determined hereafter.

Var, Vag, etc. The Sháh Námah, with a proper Aryan disregard of the contrasted sounds of a and z, reproduces Valerian's name as برانوش.

برانوش جنگي بقلب اندرون   گرفتار شد با دلی پر ز خون
و ز آن رومیان کشته شد سه هزار   ببالوینه در صف کارزار
هزار و دو سیصد گرفتار شد   دل رومیان پر ز تیمار شد

Tabari's Persian version does not give the designation of the Roman captive.

TRANSCRIPT OF PEHLVI INSCRIPTION NO. V. IN MODERN PERSIAN.

1 .... زي شهپوهري ملكان [ملكا] لسماي و هشاتري هريتن

2 ......سار شهپوهري ملكان ملكا كرتي هريتن زي من بيدون

3 .... وير... رونك هامرومري پون مگوستن كامكاري

4 .... شتري گيراك ول گيراك كبير كرتكان زي

5 .... پاتهشتري هتيمون و اوهرمزدي و يزدان

6 ...... شهپوهري ملكان ملكا پون و زلسپرهركن پكدون و بيدون

7 .... و زتي پاتهشتر و ماتيدان مي ولي

8 .... نفشي يكريمونت ايد لتير زي ايهريست

9 .... نسانم اوهرمزدي ملكان ملكا كوراپي

10 ......لي پون .. ..ان زي يزدان هسرونكي كامكاريتري

11 .... ول شتري گيراك ول گيراك كبير

12 ... و كزش هنوران ... پاتهشتري

13 .... گيراك ول گيراك كرتي .... هنا اركون

14 ....يل لسپ و زرونست ,... .ان منوان

15 .... ان مسا زك ه يونكي پون

16 .... يزدان همزون .. كامكاري

17 .... كرتكان زي ي... افزاريهي و كبير اتشي

Inscription No. V.

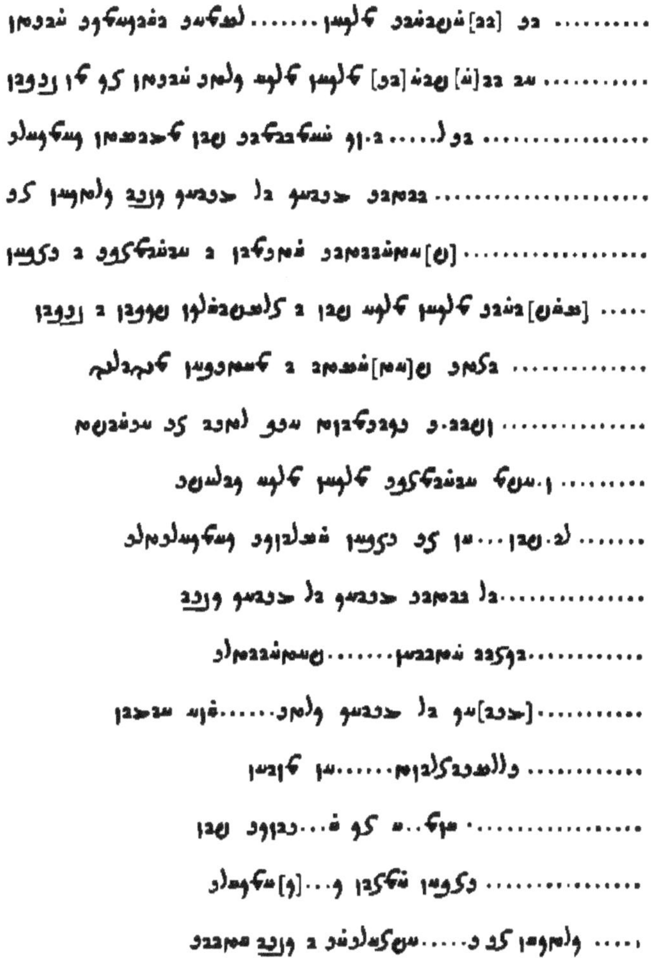

18 . . . . يف . . هشتر . . . هتيموندريتي

19 . . . .

20 . . . .

25 . . . .

27 . . . .

29 . . . .

30 . . . . و ارزديسي گركان يهي

31 . . . . . . ول گيراك كبير كرتكان زي يزدان افداديهى

32 . . . . شتري هتيمونت و زتي ا.لهشتري

33 . . . . كري . . برهست روبان و لهلن زي . . . . ميريست

34 . . . . زف كبير اتشان ويـــ وني بين شتري

35 . . . . يكم . . . وزركان

36 . . . . اتري اتشي

37 . . . .

40 . . . .

63 . . . .

64 . . . .

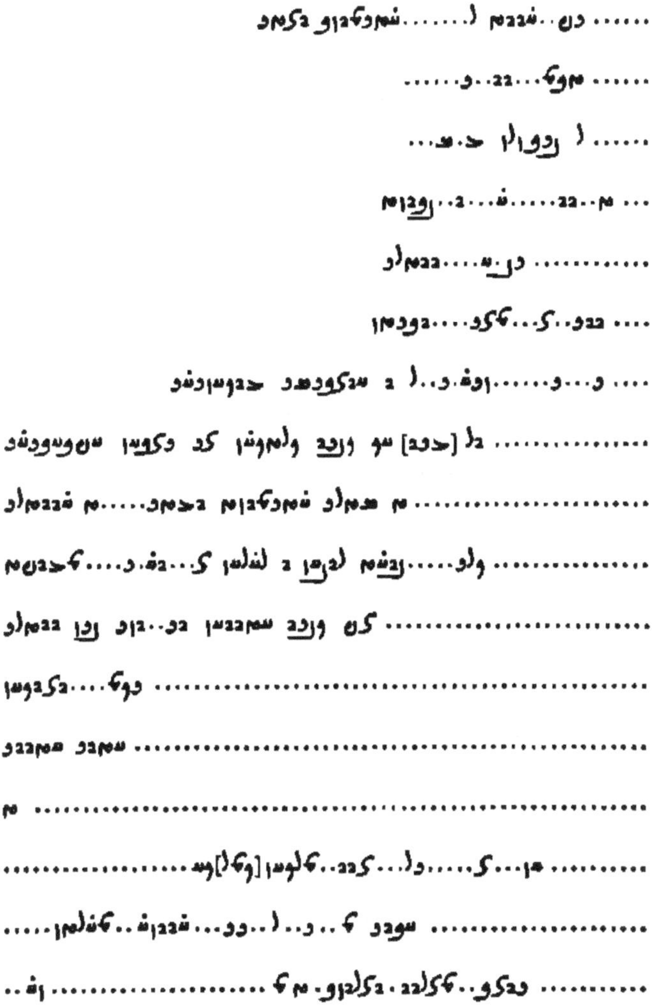

Inscription No. VI.

The celebrated bilingual Inscription of Sapor, in the Hájí-ábád cavern, seems to have been first made known to the modern world by Ker Porter, whose description of the position and surroundings of the fellow tablets is as follows:—

"The valley, or rather dell of Hájí-ábád, cannot be more than two miles in extent from end to end; the most western extremity being formed by the rocks of Nakshi-Rustam, which stretch three miles from the village of Hájí-ábád, in a direction north, 68° west. . . . . I was shewn a piece of antiquity in one of these caves, which I believe has not hitherto been noticed. It lies about a mile, nearly north, from the village. The entrance is exceedingly lofty; and within, the cavern is still more so. We see that nature originally formed it of an immense height and depth; but not satisfied with her amplitude, manual labour has added fifty yards of excavation in the vaulted roof. Along the right side, we found several square places hewn in the rock; two, nearest the entrance, at about six or seven feet from the floor of the cave, were filled with inscriptions, both were in the Pehlvi character, not much injured, but widely differing from each other; one consists of sixteen lines, the other of fourteen. I copied them with all the accuracy in my power, being much impeded by the height and darkness of their position. One portion of the three upper lines I could not make out in the least. Each inscription occupies a whole excavated tablet of about four feet in width."

Sir Ephraim Stannus's direct plaster casts of these inscriptions, taken from the face of the living rock, were brought to Europe and published in the form of jumbled and imperfect engravings, among the Transactions of the Royal Society of Dublin in 1835. The former obviously authentic reproductions of the original very early attracted the attention of Mr. Norris, who promptly devoted himself to their decipherment, for which De Sacy's essays on kindred texts had already in a measure paved the way. The interpretation of these new documents, however, proved a more serious task than had been anticipated, and Mr. Norris, in the self-denying hope[1] that some of the then more advanced Zend students might be in a condition to supply us with tentative translations, prepared with his own hand accurate pentagraph copies of the bilitural texts, which were eventually prefixed by Westergaard to his edition of the Bundehesh,[2] but no analysis or preliminary commentary was attempted on this occasion; nor has that author, in his subsequent introduction to the Zend Avesta,[3] made any seeming advance in satisfying himself of the meaning or contents of these writings, beyond the detection of the single word بريتان,[4] which Anquetil had already determined from other sources. A similar reserve has been maintained by Dr. F. Spiegel, who has given us so excellent a work on the Pârsi language,[5] as well as a series of Essays, of far higher pretensions, on the Huzvâresch-Sprache.[6] Dr. Martin Haug, indeed, was the only one of the prominent Zend scholars of that day who attempted to face the real difficulties of the interpretation, or who dared to venture beyond the safe limits, which the parallel Greek translations secured for the explanation of the opening passage, detailing the conventionally verbose titles and descent of the king.

Dr. Haug's first effort appeared in 1854.[7] A more extended analysis is to be found in his work published in Bom-

[1] I myself had very much to thank Mr. Norris for in those early days of our joint interest in Pehlvi decipherment. See J.R.A.S. (1849), vol. xii. p. 263; Num. Chron. (1849), xii. p. 72.
I do not seek the slightest reserve in alluding to my own limited objects and contracted application of the documents in question in 1849. My studies, at the moment, merely extended to a definition of the normal forms of the lapidary letters with a view to aid the determination of the contracted outlines of the cognate characters on the coins I happened to be engaged upon. See J.R.A.S. (1849), vol. xii. pp. 263-5-8, etc.; Num. Chron. (1849), p. 72, *et seq.*

[2] The Bundehesh. N. L. Westergaard. Copenhagen, 1851. Professor Westergaard had previously directly copied the original inscriptions themselves during the course of a tour in Persia, and some of his foot notes and corrections are of considerable value.

[3] Zend Avesta, "The Zend Texts." Vol. I. Copenhagen, 1852-54.

[4] Pp. 18, 21.

[5] Grammatik der Pârsisprache. Leipzig, 1851.

[6] Grammatik der Huzvâresch-Sprache. Vienna, 1856. Die Traditionelle Literatur der Parsen. Vienna, 1860.

[7] Über die Pehlewi-Sprache und den Bundehesh. Göttingen, 1854, p. 5.

bay in 1862,[1] and a far more imposing array of critical identifications is inserted in his introduction to Hoshengji-Jamaspji's *Farhang-i-oim-yak*, 1867.[2] In conclusion, the writer announces that he hopes soon to publish a full "translation and explanation of both texts" of the inscription.[3] I must frankly admit that my system of reading and interpretation varies materially from that of Dr. Haug, so that I labour under the disadvantage, as an amateur learner, of differing at the outset from a practised professional teacher; but as there is no antagonism in the matter, but merely an independent search after knowledge in either case, I trust we shall speedily arrive at a translation that will satisfy ourselves and, I regret to say, the very limited circle of those who take an interest in these studies.

As regards the materials for the reconstruction of correct texts of the two inscriptions at present available, I may mention that Sir E. Stannus's casts of the Sassanian version stop short with the sixth out of the total of sixteen lines. The Chaldæo-Pehlvi text is complete in its full fourteen lines, but the plaster impressions have been taken in four separate squares, which have, as a rule, suffered greatly on the edges, and supply a very imperfectly connected line either at the horizontal or cross perpendicular points of junction (see the Photograph). The British Museum copies are in better condition than those of the Royal Asiatic Society, while we may reasonably infer that the Dublin impressions are the best of all. Ker Porter's artistic facsimiles are of great use occasionally, and M. Flandin's more labored reproductions, at times supply the correct forms of dubious letters. I have also at my disposal a worn and nearly obliterated pencil copy of the entire Sassanian text made by Sir H. Rawlinson, who, however, omitted to secure a new facsimile of the counterpart Chaldæan.

[1] Essays on the Sacred Language, Writings, and Religion of the Parsees. Bombay, 1862.

[2] An old Zand-Pahlavi Glossary, by Destur Hoshengji-Jamaspji, High Priest of the Parsis in Malwa, with notes and introduction by Dr. M. Haug. London, 1867.

[3] Pp. xx. xxi.

Hajiabad Inscription, No. VI.

The opening word in either version of this inscription is defined in the plural form, in seemingly intentional contrast to the singular number, made use of on ordinary occasions, where the writing avowedly refers to an isolated individual in a given group of sculpture, or to a general composition, wherein the leading figure alone is indicated. In the present instance, the text must be supposed to advert to the general series of illustrations of Sapor's deeds delineated in the bas-reliefs in immediately proximate localities; or, probably, to some special mural representation of the mundane and higher powers more directly referred to in the text, which may have been either only preliminarily designed, partially executed, or afterwards intentionally destroyed.[1] The duplicate legends in parallel cases commence severally with פתכר and پتكري. In this epigraph פתכלין the Chaldæan plural is found in one version, and پتكلاي in the other, which seemingly represents a vague definition of the corresponding modern Persian *neuter plural* ها, with the connecting *izáfat* attached. The specific term itself has, for long past, been identified with the modern پيكر, S. प्रतिकार, Armenian and Aramæan, *Patkar*, "imago."

زني appears to connect itself with the Persian cuneiform *zana*,[2] the modern *Zan*, "a woman," but which in early times retained its leading signification as directly derived from a

[1] It is not easy to determine, with the limited information available, in what condition the three other tablets, ranging in line with these inscriptions within the cave, were found. There is nothing to show whether the rough surface was merely levelled and prepared, the tablets actually sculptured in relief or engraved in letters; or, on the other hand, whether the finished work was finally damaged or destroyed. M. Flandin's account of the walls of the interior is as follows:—"Ils se trouvent au Nord-ouest des monticules qui indiquent le périmètre de l'ancienne ville d' *Istakhr* et près du village d' Hadji-abad. Dans une gorge de la montagne on aperçoit des cavernes naturelles. Dans l'une d'elles sont disposées, sur sa paroi même, cinq tablettes dont deux sont revêtues d' inscriptions pehlvis bien conservées."—Flandin, p. 155, folio, texte; octavo, texte, vol. ii., p. 138.

[2] Rawlinson, J. R. A. S. x. 320; xii. 432. Oppert, J. A. 1851, pp. 564, 572, *dahyunâm paruzanânâm*, "des pays très peuplés." Anquetil, ii. 505, has *Zana* = تخم, "germe, semence, noyau." *Cf.* also जीव्, ΖΑΩ, *zîstan* زيستن, etc.

THE HAJIABAD INSCRIPTION.

The leading text in the subjoined reproduction of the inscription, in the modern Hebrew type, is a transcript of the original Chaldæo-Pehlvi version. But it must be borne in mind that the local alphabet was altogether deficient in the several Hebrew letters ט, ע, צ, ק, *and* ש.

The parallel Persian type embodies the Sassanian Pehlvi text, or the counterpart inscription in the old Pehlvi character, the sixteen lines of which have been arranged to accord as nearly as possible with the associate sentences of the fourteen lines of the Western writing. In this case also, in applying any test of modern languages, it must be understood that the old Sassanian alphabet consisted of eighteen signs in all, one of which represented both ر *and* و *; while another, the double* ي*, has been superseded in more advanced systems. The several forms of* ش, چ, ح, خ, ذ, ژ, ص, ض, ط, ظ, ع, غ, ف, *and* ق, *were therefore altogether non-existent in the then developed power of expression of this alphabet.*

1 פתכלין זניי לי מזדין אלהא שהיפוהר
1 پتکلاهي زني لي مزديسن بگي شهپوهري

2 מלכין מלכא אריאן ו אנאריאן מנו שיהר מן
2 ملکان ملکا ايران و انيران منو چتري من

3 יאותן ברי מזדין אלהא ארתחשתר מלכין מלכא
3 يزتان بري مزديسن بگي ارتهشتر ملکان ملکا

4 אריאן מנו שיהר מן יאותן פוהריפוהר בג פאפך
4 ايران منو چتري من يزتان نپي بگي پابکي

5 מלכא ו אמת לן זניי הרדיא שדית חדמתיי השתרדרין
5 ملکا اپن امت زني هتبا شديتن اديني لرمني شتردران

6 ברביתאן רבאן ו אנאתן שדית ו נגלי פתן זניי וים
6 وبربيتان و ويرکان و اناتن شدبتن اپن لگلي پون زني دوني

7 החאימות ו הדדיא להדלהו שיתי לברא רמית ברא
7 هنهتون اين هتيا لجدرزك چيتان لبرا رميتن برا

8 תמיי אנו הדדיאן פלהלהו ינבאתר יילא יהות איכ
8 ولي و ياكاين هتيا رميتن تمي وياك زك اركون لايهوت ايک

9 אך שיתי בנית התגרי כללברא שרדדא אכמי יהות
9 هت چيتان چيتي هوي ادت بيروني بتياك يهوت

10 התגרי אכין לן אופרשת מנו שיתי פנייסתר
10 هوي اهر لني نرمات منو چيتاي ارلندلي

11 בנית אס מנו ידא הרוב הינת נגלו פתן
11 چيتي منو يدي نب هوي زك لكلي پون

12 זניי וים היף החאימור ו הדדיא כלהו
12 زني نوني ايو هنهتون و هتيا ولزك

13 שיתי היף שדי ו מנו הדדיא כלהו שיתי
13 چيتاني ايو شديتن اهر منو چتيا ولزك چيتان

14 יא מוד להוף ידא רוב הדדין
14 رميتن ولي ليدي نب

root in common with the Sanskrit जन् "to be born," जन "man, individually or collectively, mankind," etc. In the present inscription it appears to carry the double sense of the *person* (of Sapor) in this place, and subsequently in زني‌دوني, for *people* of the world, in the same manner as تن in Persian is primarily the *body*, and secondarily, as in تني چند, "some *people*."

The לי, لي in the position it here occupies or in its subsequently curtailed form can scarcely represent anything but the grammatical ל, the recognised Semitic sign of the dative, which was so often employed to mark the genitive case.

בג *Baga* and بگي *Bagi*, "divine," are manifest in their derivation and meaning, as is the Chaldæan בְּרִי = بري, "a son" (from בְּרָא, "to form, to create"), which coincides in both versions. The contrast between the פוהרי פוהר [पुत्रपुत्र], "son's son," and the نپي *Nepos* (نبيره), "a grandson," of the associate Sassanian text is curious, and a like discrimination is observed elsewhere in these inscriptions, while an earlier parallel of a similar term is to be found in the Cuneiform *Nayaka*, "grandfather" (J.R.A.S. xv. 160).

There is nothing that need detain us in the formal repetition of the ordinary series of titles till we come to the conjunction و in line five, which is represented in the fellow text by the word اپن (the Hebrew and Chaldee אַף, Syriac ܐܦ, Arabic فَ, "also," "besides," etc.). The next words, אמת and امت, clearly stand for the Arabic أُمَّة, "coetus, multitudo" (the obsolete Hebrew אָמַם, "to collect," "to congregate"), which aptly falls in with the succeeding زني. The adventitious לן of the Western version is possibly the ordinary לי affected by Pehlvi leanings towards superfluous *núns*.[1]

הודיא and دنيا I have already suggested to have been

[1] For many years past I have been in the habit of representing these superfluous ן's, or final Pahlvi *núns*, by the modern Arabic sign of *sukún* ـْ, "a pause," or an indication that no short vowel existed in the preceding consonant, under the impression that these mute finals in Pehlvi had something essentially in common with the characteristic home-speech of the Aryans, which originated the Cuneiform

earlier and continuously existent forms of the Pehlvi كدي, King, the خدا of the later writings, which eventually reverted to its primary signification of the name of the Almighty among the Muhammadans, each and all of which terms seem to have a derivation in common with the Cuneiform Ḥaldia (Ḥ'aldia).[1]

But a more ample and extended identification of the divergent varieties of the same designation may be followed in Ἄλδος and Ζεὺς Ἀλδήμιος (בעלחלדים) on the one part,[2] and the אחד *unus*, חדד, Ἀδάδ, Ἀράδ, Ἀδάρ, Χοδδάν, Χουδάν, on the other: in the latter case it is proved from independent sources that the original name of the Sun (God) descended to the King in an almost natural course as the highest of earthly authorities.[3]

\ or "sign of disjunction" (J.R.A.S. x. 173), that so distinctly declared itself the Archæmenian amalgamation of the literal signs and subsidiary adaptation of the clay-penmanship of Mesopotamia. Viewed under the former aspect the Pehlvi *sán* would seem to hold duties in common with the Sanskrit ् *virâma*, which indicated, in that grammatical system, a suppression of the short vowel *a* otherwise inherent in all ordinary consonants.

As far as I have been able to detect amid the mists of Pehlvi epigraphy there is no apparent grammatical purpose in the irregular addition of this concluding ȷ among the coin legends; its employment, indeed, seems to have been simply phonetic and curiously arbitrary in its application. It may, perchance, have had something to do with the ancient notion of emphasis, which the more definite isolation of a word would itself in a manner secure (see Oppert, J.A. (1857), pp. 143–4). At times these ȷ's were clearly used for the simple purpose of barring a possible conjunction of letters that were not intended to be coupled or run into each other, as in 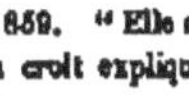 عبدوا 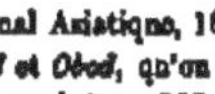 عبدولعزيزي. Abdulaziz-i-Abdala.—J.R.A.S. xii. 304.

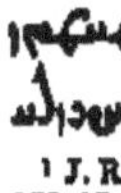 (محمد / ي ابدوا) Muhammad-i-Abdala.—J. R. A. S. xiii. 411.

[1] J. R. A. S. ix. 388, 405–6, 410, 413; Jour. Asiatique, 1836, p. 14; 1864, pp. 173, 174.

[2] Renan, Journal Asiatique, 1859. "Elle se retrouve peut-être dans les divinités arabes *Aud* et *Obod*, qu'on croit expliquer par عوض ou عود et ابوعوض tempus, pater temporis." p. 268.

[3] Selden, De Diis Syris, 1662, p. 176; Renan, J.A. 1859, pp. 266, 267; Ἄδωδος βασιλεὺς θεῶν, 268 and 273; Kitto's Cyclopædia of Bible Lit. and Smith's Dict. of the Bible, *sub voce*, *Hadad*; Josephus, vii. 2; viii. 6.

The king's worldly position and exalted pretensions towards a subdued God-

שדית and شديش present no difficulties in the obvious root شَدّ and the numerous derivative associations of ancient speech to be found in שַׁדַּי, "the Almighty," in the sense of "power," etc. In the same way اديني, accepting the Sassanian as the leading version, falls in completely with אדני, from אָדֹן, אָדוֹן, "Lord," אֲדֹנָי, "my lord," which we retain in our own conventional tongue in the derivative Ἄδωνις we learnt from the Greeks.[1] The Semitic חורמתי from خَدَمَ may, perhaps, be understood in the higher sense of the recipient of service,[2] rather than in the later acceptation of the word, as خدمت, "service." We may here pause for a moment to mark the contrasted dialects of the joint versions in the use of the Semitic genitive prefix ל in the one case and the employment of the Persian Izáfat in the other.

The series of words رمني line five, רמית = رميتن line seven, and رميتن in lines eight and fourteen, have clearly a common origin in the root רוּם,[3] "to be exalted." Abundant parallels of the same ruling idea are to be found in the Bible phraseology in עליון (from עָלָה, "to ascend"), שָׁמַיִם (from שָׁמָה, سَمَا, "to be high"). While the derivative examples are familiar to our ears in "Rimmon, Ramah, Ramoth-Gilead," etc.

The השתרדרין and شتردران in their absolute identity of

head had equally a fair analogy with and a simultaneous teaching in the conventional use of the mundane term for king, which was so often applied in its higher sense to the Divine power in the patriarchal ages. So that, in effect, the reigning king, the Ἄναξ ἀνδρῶν, without any conception of unduly approaching the true God, was, in effect, next to God upon earth; just as THE GOD of early thought was, under the worldly idea, only the self-created supreme king. The "My King and my God," of David's prayer (Ps. v. 2), finds numerous parallels throughout Scripture. "The LORD is king for ever and ever." "Save LORD: let the king hear us when we call" (Ps. x. 16; xx. 9). See also xliv. 4; xlvii. 2, 6, 7; xlviii. 2; Proverbs xxiv. 21; Isaiah viii. 21; xxxiii. 22. "I AM the LORD, your Holy One, the Creator of Israel, your King," xliii. 15; Zech. xiv. 9; Malachi i. 14.

[1] Renan, J.A., 1859, p. 363–4.

[2] "Veneratus est aliquem, quomodo dominum servus venerari debet."—Freytag.

[3] Dr. Haug derives these words from רְמָא, "to throw;" but רָמָה from רום, "a high place, especially consecrated to the worship of idols," seems to be a better identification.—Cf. Ῥαμᾶς ὁ ὕψιστος θεός. "Hadad-rimmon." Selden, ii. 10. Movers. Phœn. i. 196.

meaning, and but slightly varied transliteration and plural discriminations require but scant comment, and point with sufficient distinctness to the immemorial office of Satrap, which constituted so essential an element of Persian administration. The بربيتان in like manner is as little open to contest either with regard to the reading or general import, and without needlessly seeking for ancient identifications we may confide in the meaning the Parsis but lately attributed to the word of "Salar en chef,"[1] or some modification of an equivalent dignity.

The word وبركان is altogether indeterminate in the existing copies of the original, but its Chaldæan counterpart רבאן sufficiently attests its primary meaning, so that it is useless to speculate further upon the true form.

The closely concurring literal elements of the parallel אנאתן and اناتن would at first sight appear to identify the joint terms with the designation of *Andta*, the simple name of *Tanais* or Anahit, a divinity to whom the Achæmenians themselves confessed attachment in the days of their less severe adherence to the supremacy of Ormazd,[2] and whose worship was so far identified with degraded Zoroastranism as to secure for her an independent *Yasht* in the mixed invocations of the Zend Avesta.[3] The succeeding epithet شديتن might also be held to confirm the position it was proposed to assign to the goddess, while the attribution of the designation to a member of the ancient Chaldaic Pantheon might seem to be consecutively supported by the occurrence of the names of *Gula* (line 6), *Anu* (line 8), *Danit*, with its legitimate correspondent of '*Hpa*[4] (in line 9), and the letters which constitute so near an approach to the designation of Ishtar (יסתר, in line 10). But it will

[1] Anquetil, ii. 486. The pronunciation of the Armenian *Sbarabied*, "connétable," does not differ greatly from the Pehlvi word. See St. Martin, Mem. sur. l'Arménie, i. 298.

[2] J.R.A.S. xv. p. 159. Inscription of Artaxerxes Mnemon, p. 162. See also p. 264.

[3] Haug, "Language," etc. *Aban Yasht*, p. 176. *Ardvi Sûra Anâhita*, "high, excellent, pure."

[4] هوري may be read as هري, the ة will answer for either letter.

be seen, as the analysis of the bilingual document proceeds, that its text has nothing in common with idolatry, and that the various appellations as they occur in this inscription had, in the natural course of vernacular speech, already reverted to their primary significations, from which, in so many instances, the specific titles of the early divinities had been originally derived. Beyond this, there are otherwise grave difficulties in the way of reconciling the run of the passage with the preceding sentence, if Anahit or other local Deities are to conclude the list of the mundane officials subject to the reigning King, which sense I conceive the leading هـتيا must, of necessity, carry in this place. Though it is no easy matter to decide positively where the change from the enumeration of the titles of the Monarch to the invocation of the Divinity is effected, especially as the term هـتيا is applied in common to both; but it would seem that concurrence of the parallel *waus* (ו and و) at this point marks the want of continuity, which the اين of the Sassanian is possibly designed to indicate in other parts of the inscription,[1] and under such a view of the tenor of the epigraph, we might be justified in accepting אנאתן as an imperfect reproduction of the Chaldean אַנְתּוּן (Syriac ܐܢܬܘܢ) "Ye," in which case a translation might be suggested of "Ye Powerful" (Thou, O LORD), the plural form of the pronoun being designedly employed, as in يزدان, and in the conventional *pluralis excellentiæ* of the Hebrew and other Oriental tongues.

Next in order follow the words:

ו נגלי פתן זניי וים החאימות

ابن لگلي يون زنيِ دوني هنهـتـون

which, taking the Sassanian as the clearest text, may be rendered "also of joy among the people of the world promoting" ("and on earth peace, good will towards men," Luke ii. 14: Isaiah lvii. 19).

[1] The particle وَ is irrespective of order: فَ on the contrary distinguishes it.

The كلي may be taken to correspond with גִּילָה, "rejoicing, gladness" (from גִּיל or גּוּל, "to move in a circle).[1]

The لكلي of the Sassanian is replaced by נגליי (or, as some copies make it, נגלין) in the other version, but as the reading of كل is pretty well assured, we may disregard the defect of the initial ل in the second text, as that letter so frequently interchanged with נ. The بون and בּין, "in, among," are both clear enough, and the various responsibilities of زني I have already attempted to explain (pp. 73-76 *ante*).

دوني, which is erroneously copied as دوكي in most of the modern facsimiles, is consistently supported by the corresponding רים, and may fairly be associated with the دون, "low;" دُنيا, "the world" (אֶרֶץ, أَرْضٌ, "low;" אֶרֶץ, "the earth"), while the רים resolves itself into the Biblical עָם, "a people," in its wider sense for "all mankind."

The word החאימות seems to be derived from קוּם "to rise up" (הֵקִים, "to raise up"), the Arabic قَامَ, "stetit" (قَيَّامٌ, "subsistens, sempiternus," hence القيوم, "Deus"). The parallel term in the Sassanian Pehlvi is هنهتن, which I suppose to be the participle present of the obscure verb اناتونتن, the modern نهادن, "to place," and under such a continuative action of "placing, or who places," the meaning would be clear, as well as in the causal verb of the counterpart writing.

The joint texts proceed:

ו הרדיא להדלהו שיתי לבריא רמית בריא תמיי

اين هتيا لجدرزكت جيتان لبرا رميتن برا ولي

Also of the God of Might, the Lord[2] of the creator, the heavenly creator, the beloved.

The Chaldæo-Pehlvi version varies in the substitution of

[1] גִּיל בַּיהוָה, "to rejoice in Jehovah." Isaiah xxix. 19.—"Joyful even unto rejoicing." Job iii. 22.

[2] "The Lord said unto my Lord."—Ps. cx. 1.

להדלהו in place of لهدرزك. The הדל may either be a very imperfect transcript of the جدر (تَدَر Providentia Dei, from قَدَر potuit), or it may be an independent quotation of the عدل, justice, another of the attributes of God, with the final Arabic و corresponding with the Pehlvi زك.

One of the nearly parallel terms in these conjoint inscriptions, the root of which it is more particularly desirable to determine, is שיתי=جيتان lines 7, 9, جيتي line 11, שיתי=جيتاني and שיתי=جيتان in line 13, and הדריא=جتيا in line 13. The last of which derivatives in its textual correspondence with הדריא sufficiently indicates the sense of the entire series of doubtful words, and justifies what might otherwise be considered to be an improper manipulation of the materials of the original, with a view to suit preconceived ideas of its possible interpretation; and, indeed, but few commentators would care to hazard an approximate meaning to words so similar in form but belonging to such opposite systems of speech as شديتن and שיתי, when occurring in one and the same inscription; but those who would encounter mixed Aryan and Semitic records must hold themselves prepared for similar responsibilities at every turn.

Our latest authorities have already associated شيد with the Zend *Khshaêta* क्षि (क्षयति - ते) "to rule," hence "splendens, dominus, rex."[1] The initial ש as represented by the associate Aryan ج is quite in accord with the then existing practice, as may be seen in the concurrent מנושיהר=منوجتري, and in the name of Zoroaster, زوراد چست, in the fifteenth tablet of the Paï Kúlí Inscription. The short *i* is also in favour of the identification proposed, and the occurrence of ت in preference to the modern د is alike typical of the earlier notions of orthography.

The Chaldæo-Pehlvi accords identically with the Sassanian

[1] Vullers, *sub voce*, شيد. The word is common enough in the sense of "shining," if not something of larger import, in خورشيد ,جمشيد ,شيدة, etc. Anquetil (ii. 449) has Zend Schâthrâo = Pahlvi Farmân dâdâr; and (at p. 508), Pehlvi Scharitah = Padeschah.

in the لبرا رميتن برا but changes the concluding ولي into חמי. The former word is optionally rendered as Dominus on ordinary occasions, but the associate חמי in this place and the recurrence of the same word تمي in the next sentence in the Sassanian version seems to point to origin rather than to rank. Under such an interpretation of the passage وَلِى would revert to its leading meaning of "Valde Propinquus fuit *alicui*."[1]

The associate חמי=تمي has already been noticed (p. 40), and attributed to a source in common with the Aryan تُخم, the Zend *taokhma*, Sanskrit तोक्म, and Cuneiform *Tumá*, "granum, semen, radix."

The Creator of heaven and earth[2] is described by برا رميتن برا, about the meaning or derivation of which terms there can be little question.[3]

The next sentence contains the words

אנו הדיאן פלתלדו

و ياكاين هتيا رميتن تمي

The Anu *Haddián* I propose to connect with the אנו (a confessedly irregular form of the nominative of the pronoun אני), "I;" in the exalted sense of *ego*, as denoting the First Cause, which is symbolized in the Scriptures as "I AM THAT I AM." "I AM hath sent you." (Exod. iii. 14).[4] In the present combination the words would read, "God of other Gods." The ياكاين هتيا, of course, conveys some nearly identical meaning, and it becomes necessary to define, as far as may be, the force and origin of the frequently-recurring ياكث. With our present

[1] The word is used in a variety of senses, such as علي ولي الله, ولي عهد. وَلِى "Amicus, Dominus." مَوْلَى "Dominus, herus, item filius."

[2] Isaiah xlii. 5, xliv. 24; Jeremiah x. 12; St. Matthew xi. 25.

[3] بَرَا Creavit, ברא, "to form, to create, to produce."

[4] Exod. vi. 2, 3, 6, 29. "For I am the LORD, I change not." Malachi iii. 6.

limited knowledge of the derivation of the specific term, I am inclined to reduce it to the simple element of the Persian يكَ "one,"[1] and to suppose that it referred in its early use to the ONE Divine power, but, in progress of time, came to be conventionally accepted as a term for other gods; under these conditions the ياكاين may be taken to be an exceptional Semitic plural, and to read in sequence, "the seed of the high God of Gods."[2] The continuation of the sentence in the Chaldæo-Pehlvi, though differing in its phraseology, confirms, if it does not extend, the signification of the fellow Sassanian text. The word פלט has been associated by some of our late Cuneiform Expositors with the meaning of "race, family," etc., but without insisting upon an identification which would so singularly accord with the parallel version in this case, it may fairly be quoted as one of the possible divarications from the severe import of the original root, which is only doubtfully determined by our Lexicographers as פָּלַט, "to be smooth,"[3] "to escape," hence "to survive," and "to live;" also "to let escape, to deliver," and inferentially, "to bring forth." In another sense the derivatives carry the idea of "life," while the word פְּלָאיָה signifies "whom Jehovah makes distinguished." The concluding לדו, "of him," sufficiently declares itself.

[1] Compare Sanskrit एक "one," एकता "unity" (oneness in theology). Persian يكَ "unus," يكّه "unus, unicus," يكى "unitas," يكتائى حق "unitas Dei," يكتا "God," etc. A curious example of the definition of the first cause or supreme universal spirit, occurs on a coin of Mahmúd of Ghazni, struck at Mahmúdpúr — in the Sanskrit translation and reproduction of the Muslim لا اله الا الله وحده by the word अव्यक्तमेक, "the invisible one." The provincial version of अव्यक्तमेकम्, "the indiscrete, the invisible one." J. R. A. S., xvii. 167.

[2] أَحَدُ الأَحَدِين, "unus unorum," واحد الاحدين, etc.

[3] Arabic فَلَطَ فَلَّصَ (خَلَصَ), etc.

The next passage continues :

ינבאתר יילא יהות איכאך שיתי בנית התנרי

وياکزك ارگون ايوت ايكهت چيتان چيتي هوي

In the Sassanian—and One that, of the Archon of the Jews, sole Lord of Lords be (is).
In the C. P. version— . . . . over the Jews sole ruler, Lord created, ye (are).

Having proclaimed the divine origin of our Lord, the text next proceeds to indicate his mission upon earth. The first word in the Sassanian counterpart of this passage that requires comment is the ارگون, which can scarcely be referred to any other association than that of the Greek Ἄρχων,[1] a word which entered so largely into the gradational definitions of the later Hebrew Hierarchy.

In like manner I can hardly be mistaken in accepting the ايوت and يوت (in line 9) as the common designation of the Jewish nation at large; notwithstanding the prosthetic initial ا in the one case, or the use of the final ت in the place of the more appropriate د in both instances, a substitution which is essentially characteristic of the indifference to the proper discrimination of the two sounds inherent in ordinary Pehlvi writings.

The ايكهت, the first syllable of which is obviously the يكت, so often repeated in the general context, I have suggestively rendered in the adjective or adverbial form. چيتان چيتي is sufficiently assured and the هوي "he" has already been the subject of comment (p. 48).

The Chaldæo-Pehlvi version, as usual, is less clear than the Sassanian, the ינבאתר I have not yet succeeded in identifying; but the ילאיהות (على يوت) "over the Jews," accords sufficiently with the fellow text. The איכאך may perchance be a simple Pehlvi plural of איך, with the authorized K final in the place of the N. Though the Sanskrit एकाकी

[1] "Χριστὸς δὲ παραγενόμενος ἀρχιερεὺς τῶν μελλόντων ἀγαθῶν." Hebrews ix. 11. A considerable portion, indeed, of St. Paul's Epistle to the Hebrews is devoted to the affirmation of this title of High Priest, and to the explanation of its import and bearing upon the old Law. See ii. 17; iii. 1, 2, 6; iv. 14, 15; v. 5, 6, 10; vi. 20; vii. 1, 2, 3, 15, 16, 21, 26, 27, 28; viii. 1, 2, 3, 6; x. 21; xiii. 11, 12.

ekáki, "alone," manifestly affords a preferable parallel to the associate passage in the Sassanian.

My greatest difficulty in this sentence, I am free to confess, consists in the word בנית; any severe reduction of the term to the rules of Hebrew grammar would manifestly be out of place in the present agglomeration of many tongues, so that probably the best solution that can at present be offered is to understand the derivative in the proper and widely diffused sense of the original root بَنَا, "struxit, ædificavit, condidit;" and to look upon the בנית in this sentence as bearing the sense of "created," (Arabic, بِنْيَة, "a thing constructed, a building," etc.);[1] but I feel that I am treading upon delicate ground, though, under any circumstances, the contrast between "The BUILDER" (or Creator) and the final *Edifice*, whether the latter be symbolized under the terms, Son, Son of Man, *Branch*,[2] house, foundation,[3] or the typical *buildings* of the later writings,[4] all in their degree fall under the self-same original metaphor, and all revert in their subordinate leading details either directly or indirectly to the MAKER and *the thing made*; so that in the present instance the less any particular definition is forced amid so obvious a succession of simple meanings, the more safely we may proceed to test what remains of the larger problem yet to be established. But on looking more closely into the general question, it will be seen that there are traces of a direct motive and intention

[1] A similar course of developement occurs in the parallel cases of خَلَقَ "procreavit," خَالِق, "Creator," خَلِيقَة, "creata res" (Homines), بَرَأَ, "creavit," بَرِيَّة, "creatura."

[2] Isaiah xi. 1; Jeremiah xxiii. 5, 6. "For, behold, I will bring forth my servant the BRANCH." Zechariah iii. 8, 9. "Behold the man whose name is The BRANCH." vi. 12.—Poetically, branch is son of a tree.

[3] "Foundation"—θεμέλιος—which is Jesus Christ." 1 Corinthians iii. 11.—"We have a building of God, an house not made with hands" (*οἰκοδομὴν ἐκ Θεοῦ ἔχομεν, οἰκίαν ἀχειροποίητον*). 2 Cor. v. 1.—"But he that built all things is God." Hebrews iii. 4, 6; ix. 11; xi. 10.—"In whom all the building fitly framed together, groweth unto a holy temple in the Lord." Ephes. ii. 19, 20, 21.

[4] Genesis i. 27; Isaiah xliii. 1, 7, 11; xlv. 12, 18, 18; St. John iii. 16, 18; v. 18; 1 Corinthians iii. 10, 11; Colloss. iii. 4, 10, 11; Hebrews ix. 11; xi. 17, 16.

in the reserve maintained under the avowedly open term "created," inasmuch as with Oriental feelings on the subject of women, and the degraded position assigned to them as household goods, a difficulty would at any time present itself with regard to their part in so divinely inspired an event; indeed, the birth of Our Saviour was one of the special points upon which the Eastern mind was altogether abroad and incompetent to understand, hence the earliest discussions on the subject at once introduced discord into their section of the church.[1] It will have been noticed that the parallel texts of the Inscription are careful to avoid the use of the term "Son" in reference to Our Lord, though Sapor is freely defined as "Son," and "Son's Son;" but the ولي, تمي, and פלות, which appeared, at first sight, to be undue shortcomings, seem to have been, in reality, guarded and designed limitations, which consistently coincide with the idea of direct and special "*creation* by the Almighty," without entering too definitely into the mode or method, which would be incomprehensible to and far beyond the range of average local thought.

There are serious obstacles in the way of any conclusive determination of the value of the word הרתגרי, which it will

[1] Here is a statement of the case as given by Tabari: "Quand la religion de Jésus fut très-repandue, Eblis fit son apparition, et un jour de fête, lorsqu'un grande nombre d'hommes, sectateurs de Jésus, était réuni dans le temple de Jérusalem, il s'y présenta accompagné de deux Divs" (saying) "nous avons voulu entendre ce que vous dites concernant Jésus. Les hommes répondirent: Jésus est le prophète, l'esprit de Dieu et le fils de Marie; il n'a pas été engendré par père. Je pense que Dieu est le père de Jésus. L'un des Divs dit: Cette parole est un non-sens, car Dieu n'a pas d'enfants et n'a pas commerce avec une femme; mais Jésus c'est Dieu même, qui est descendu du ciel et est entré dans le sein de Marie; il en est sorti pour se montrer aux hommes, sous la forme d'un homme, puis il est retourné au ciel, car Dieu a le pouvoir d'être où il veut et de montrer aux hommes ce qu'il veut. L'autre Dîv dit . . . et il l'a établi au milieu des hommes comme un signe (de sa toute puissance); puis il s'est associé Jésus et Marie, afin qu'ils fussent honorés à l'égal de Dieu. . . . Alors les Chrétiens se divisèrent en trois sectes, dont chacune accepta l'une de ces trois doctrines."—Tabari, M. Zotenberg, i. p. 566. So also Abgar, in his letter to Our Saviour, evidently leant to the first conception, "either that thou art God, and having descended from heaven," in preference to the alternative, "or else doing them, thou art the Son of God." Eusebius, Eccl. Hist. i. 13; Moses of Khorene (French edit.) cap. xxxi.; Bayer, Hist. Osrhoena, p. 105; Ancient Syriac Documents, W. Cureton, London, 1861, p. 2.

be seen runs parallel to the Sassanian هوي. In the first place it is not by any means beyond possibility that they may both be verbs, the one from the Chaldæan הֲוָה and הֲוָא "to be," the other from the Persian هستن "to be." (هستند) An objection likewise exists to a too ready acceptance of the התגדי in the sense of "ye," as it would appear that another form of the second person plural of the pronoun had already been used in an earlier portion of this inscription (אנארתן line 6); however this argument need not unconditionally condemn the identification, as either one form or the other is sufficiently irregular, as is the nominative אנו itself, and the inscription in its several parts varies considerably in its current provincialisms.[1] But singular to say, the evidence to sustain the proposed interpretation is contributed by a second inconsistency in the very body of the text, where (in line 11) we find the word הינת, associated with the same هوي—the former of which obviously suggests the Arabic أَنْتَ "thou" as the התגדי seems to fall into some vernacular adaptation of the Arabic (feminine) plural أَنْتُنَّ "you" (אַתֵּנָה אַתֵּן "you").

כלכרא שרדדא אכמי יהות התגדי

ادت بيروني بـــتـــيـــاك يهوت هوي

C. Pehlevi.—The powerful . . . of the chosen Jews ye (are).
Sassanian.—The Supreme Lord of the Jews outside the (ancient) rites, he (is).

The opening word in this sentence requires both comment and justification, the crude ادت of the text I suppose to represent the now conventional عادة, "custom, usage, rite," etc. In most of the modern facsimiles the final ت has been resolved into two independent letters (ين), which would convert the original into the word ادين; but this severance of the component elements of a single letter is an error of frequent and almost natural recurrence among those who were either ignorant of the true forms of the character, or set themselves to trace

[1] *E.g.* especially in the conjunctions و، اين، اهر. There are other indications, likewise, of an interval having occurred between the endorsement or preparation of the introductory portions and the conclusions of these proclamations.

words to which they could not assign a meaning. The present rectification is, however, sufficiently supported by Flandin's design.

It is scarcely possible to be mistaken in the Persian individuality of the word بیرون, "outside, exterior," which in its multifarious combinations enters so largely into the home-speech of the land of which Persepolis was once the metropolis; and within whose local circuit, in secluded crypts and caverns, the present epigraphs have been so strangely preserved.

The پت‌پاك is a title of more doubtful allegiance; its value, in connexion with the frequent reiteration of one of its compound terms, within the limits of this brief record, should fully suffice to determine its second element, while the ever present پت of the contemporary Inscriptions in less adulterated Pehlvi, establishes *à priori*, a definite suggestion and understanding of the Eastern *Pati* (पतिः). A somewhat similar compound under our Western adaptation is well-known and uniformly identified with the Patriarchs of the Christian Church. I do not seek to decide upon either one or the other derivation. I have only to reconcile in this place the possible want of discrimination by either party of the *true* origin of such closely approximating sounds; but it is singular that Masaudi should have affirmed that the Christians derived all their clerical titles and designations from the Sabæans of Harran (الصابئة من الحرانيين),[1] though he honestly retains the dubious *r* in البطرك, which alone creates any difficulty in the present

[1] French edition, vol. I., p. 198. "Les Sabéens de Harran, qui ne sont que les disciples grossiers des Grecs, et la lie des philosophes anciens, ont établi dans leur temples une hiérarchie de prêtres qui correspond aux neuf sphères; le plus élevé porte le nom de *Ras Koumra* (chef des prêtres, ריש כומריא). Les chrétiens, qui leur ont succédé, ont conservé dans la hiérarchie ecclésiastique l'ordre institué par la secte sabéenne. . . la neuvième celle de *mitran* (مطران), ce qui veut dire chef de la ville (métropolitain). Enfin au-dessus de tous ces grades est celui de *batrik* (بطرك), c'est-à-dire le père des pères (patriarche). . . Telle est l'opinion des chrétiens instruits relativement à cette hiérarchie. . . . Il est hors de doute que les chrétiens ont emprunté l'idée première de cette hiérarchie aux Sabéens et que le *kasis* (القسيس), le *chamas* (الشماس) etc. sont dus à l'influence des Manichéens.—Masaudi, cap. viii.

identification; while, on the other hand, Moses of Khorene specifically reproduces the *Ptiachkh* as simply "Prince" (i. 159).[1]

The opening terms of the Chaldæo-Pehlvi counterpart of this passage are obscure, the leading word inconveniently occurs at the cross junction of our plaster casts, and the British mason has studiously adjusted the edges for the sake of the frontage, but to the clear detriment of the impressed letters. Westergaard himself seems to have had some doubt about the state of the characters as they now stand on the surface of the rock, and is, moreover, rather vague in his attempted rectification of Mr. Norris's pentagraph. The succeeding שודריא,[2] with so many analogies around it, would present no difficulties with an ascertained leader, whether substantive or adjective; but about the following אכמי there can be small matter of contest, as the separated sect declares itself outside, or as having abandoned the ancient rites; that is, as being "without the law," in the one case[3]—here it is more specific in claiming a special pre-eminence as "chosen," اخصّ (خاصّ, خصّ) special, select, most peculiar,[4] a selection

[1] "Vagharchag institue, pour gouverner de la partie nord, cette grande et puissante race: le titre de la principauté est Ptiachkh (prince) des Coucaratzi."—Mos. Khor. vol. i. p. 159; ii. 13, 169.

Visconti, Iconographie Grecque ii. 353. Onyx Gem in the Imp. Cabinet:

ΟΥΣΑΣ ΠΙΤΙΑΞΗΣ ΙΒΗΡΩΝ ΚΑΡΧΗΔΩΝ.

Ousas, Prince d'Ibérie (des Ibères Carchédiens).

"Le prince a des boucles d'oreilles à la manière orientale, une longue chevelure artistement arrangé en nattes suivant l'usage des rois perses de la dynastie des Sassanides," etc.

[2] This is possibly the Hebrew סָדַר, Chaldee סַדֵּר, "to set in a row, order," and Syriac ܣܕܪܐ, "ordo, series," "schola, liber," etc.

[3] 1 Corinthians ix. 20: "And unto the Jews I became as a Jew, that I might gain the Jews; to them that are under the law, as under the law, that I might gain them that are under the law; 21. To them that are without law, as without law (being not without law to God, but under the law to Christ), that I might gain them that are without law." (Τοῖς ἀνόμοις ὡς ἄνομος, μὴ ὢν ἄνομος Θεῷ, ἀλλ' ἔννομος Χριστῷ, ἵνα κερδήσω ἀνόμους). See also Romans ii. 14, 17; vi. 14; vii. 4, 6; x. 4; Galatians ii. 16, 19; iii. 10, 11, 12, 13, "Christ hath redeemed us from the curse of the law," 19, 23, 24; iv. 5; v. 18, etc.

[4] Ὑμεῖς δὲ γένος ἐκλεκτὸν κ.τ.λ. . . . 9 "But ye are a chosen generation, a royal priesthood, a holy nation, a peculiar people . . . 10 which in time past

the succeeding word indicates to have been directly from among the ranks of God's ancient people.

אכין לן אופרשת מנו שיתי פנייכתר
اهر لني فرمـات منوجـيتاي اولندلي

C. Pehlvi.—Of a certainty, the Master, the divine Lord, etc., etc.
Sassanian.—And, of a certainty, the Master, the divine Lord.

One of the most curious instances of the mixture of tongues in the whole of the parallel inscriptions is contributed by the word اهر, which is incontestably proved by its association with و, in line 13, to stand for nothing but the conjunction "and"; while its derivation is declared in the Sanskrit एव, *eva*; the Hindustáni اور, Bengáli আর, etc.

لني is shown by its counterpart אכין[1] (يَقِين, certa cognitio), to be the Arabic انّ *inna*, "certainly," with the prefixed ل. The فرمات *Firmáta*, has already been met with repeatedly (p. 38, etc.), and its correspondent אופרשת, though looking so strange in its Semitic clothing, is equally attributable to Aryan ethnography, and accords with the Sanskrit उपदेष्टृ *Upadeshṭri*, "one who points out, who orders, or advises."[2] The منو, "Divine" in منوجيتاي is of constant occurrence in these Sassanian epigraphs, and needs no new elucidation. The اولندلي I have, of necessity, a difficulty about, more especially as the synonym in the other text is even less positive. It might be suggested, with considerable reserve, that the former may possibly have been a compound of the Arabic أوّل, "*primum*," with the Persian دلي from دل, "the heart," as in the modern term رحمدل, "merciful," etc., but such an explanation is scarcely satisfactory; and a

were not a people, but are now the people of God; which had not obtained mercy, but now have obtained mercy." Epistle of Peter, ii. 9, 10.

[1] I myself at first read this word as *Adin*, but the foot-curve in the plaster-casts is indeterminate, and I observe that both Norris and Westergaard reject the sign of the ד altogether.

[2] उपदेष्टा *Upadeshṭá*, "*A Guru*," "a spiritual guide," from उप + दिश्, "to shew," with affix तृच्. A nearly similar sound is found in उपद्रष्टृ, "a superior," from दृश्, "to see."

combination that should include the reduction of اولندلي into اولندري, "as first in rank,"[1] in parallelism with the conversion of פנ״מרר into the Sanskrit परमेष, "supreme,"[2] however removed from the ordinary laws of interpretation, would, perhaps, better satisfy the requirements of the general context.

בינת אום מנן יראו תרוב הינת

جبتي ... منو يدي نب هوي زكث

C. Pehlvi.—Created Jesus of divine aid, THE Lord, thou
Sassanian.—Lord (Jesus) of divine aid, (*the*) Lord, he

The eleventh line of the Chaldæo-Pehlvi legend commences with the repetition of the word בנית already adverted to. In this instance the designation responds, in the order of sequence, to the جبتي of the conjoint Sassanian version. Immediately following the former of these words, in its own lapidary context, we find in clear and definitely-formed letters, and in full integrity and isolation, on the surface of the recent plaster casts of the still extant original, the *three* letters constituting the name of OUR SAVIOUR.

Of these three literal signs, the two *quasi* vowels, or, properly, mere *carrying* consonants of the Semitic system, are entirely dependent upon the true vowel sounds appropriate to the written word; but in these periods of undeveloped grammar such subdued but highly important elements of speech were altogether unprovided with definite graphic exponents.

Under such reservation as regards later and more elaborated schemes of orthography, many versions of the test letters אום might be suggested, but the most simple and obvious of them would still revert to a very exact counterpart of the name of JESUS, whether out of its many declared varieties we select the Hebrew or the Greek series of definitions. Amid all the various adaptations of the old יְהוֹשֻׁעַ whether JOSHUA, JESHUA, JOSUE, JESU, عيسى or Ἰησοῦς, there is still the same basis in

[1] The Armenian *der*, "Mourtzan-der" Seigneur des Mèdes.—Mos. Khor. l. 167.

[2] From परम + स्थ, "who stays" (a title applied, in the Sanskrit system, to Brahma).. *Cf.* προστάτης (πρoέστηκα).

these Persepolitan forms of the early Phœnician for the reconstruction of the *Ieusa*, or some such close similitude to the real name, that should set at rest all question upon the mere orthographical issue.[1]

It will be seen that the name is altogether wanting in the Sassanian version, and it has even been the custom of ordinary copyists to close up the words جيتي and منويدي as if no letters had ever intervened between them. But Flandin's facsimile, which has evidently been traced with a scrupulous desire for accuracy, indicates the existence of a fissure or disintegration of the surface of the rock, just at this very point, and extending downwards through the succeeding lines, while the tracing equally indicates by the distance between the two words as nearly as possible the space required for the three missing letters.

The منويدي of, so to say, both epigraphs, seems clear enough, though it may be needful to explain the preference here assigned to the translation of "*aid*" over the more common rendering of "*hand*." Persian Dictionaries draw a very nice, but seemingly just discrimination, being the singular and plural forms of one and the same word: يَدٌ is essentially "a hand," but in the sequent *rationale* of "power," the subordinate combinations extended over a very enlarged range of significations: in the Hebrew the derivatives were comparatively restricted, but in the Arabic these divarications concentrated sooner or later, in the Persian vocabularies, into the plural يُدِيّ in the leading sense of "aid, assistance, succour," and in

[1] In the adapted alphabet of the Persian Jews, made use of in the Bible Society's New Testament, the name is written ישוע. It is as well that all objections to the apparent absence of an *initial* ' or *Yod* in this unquestionably important name in the present text, should be answered in anticipation by a citation of the אכון of line ten, where the expressed *alif* initial clearly defines a simple ي or a *Yod* of Hebrew Grammar. See also the ا prosthetic in ايهوت and in ايو = ىو. On the other hand, there need be no reserve in admitting that, under the licence claimed above, the name may be converted into many other modified forms, but notably into عوص, "a sign," (or possibly עוץ &c., or even عوذ, عاذ, עוז, "refuge"). However, it is the essentially Christian characteristics and general tenor of the document that chiefly recommends the reading advocated in the text.

some cases even to the signification of "repentance" ("Pœnitentia" Freytag). The דיא of the parallel version might be quoted in support of the duplication of the final in يدوي only that this would not be altogether a safe argument in the presence of the exceptional (emphatic) דיא of the Chaldæan vernacular in Daniel v. 5, 24, though probably any such heritage had been subdued by contact with the mixed dialects of more Southern latitudes.

The word نب *Naba* would at first sight naturally suggest the obvious interpretation of "Prophet," but taken in connexion with the רוב of the counterpart transcript it will be necessary to elevate its meaning into "Lord," or a later adaptation of the ancient "Nebo," as derived from the root نَبَا, "Editus, elatus fuit,"[1] נבה, "to be prominent," and not as having any direct connexion with נָבָא, "to pour forth."

The article ה *the* prefixed to the רוב, which gives force to the parallel term, would altogether remove the joint titles far above the grade of a mere *vâtes* or "prophesier." The effect of the double letters of the current speech رَبّ and רַבָּב seems to have been sought in graphic expression by the lengthening the vowel sound of ـَ into و, as in the analogous case of ياك, which was the substitute for the dominant Arabic يكّ (the modern Persian يكّ).

The texts next reiterate the passages from lines 6, 7.

נגליי פתן זניי וים היף החאימות

لكلي پون زني دوني ايو هتهتون

C. Pehlvi.— . . well sustaining joy among the people of this world.
Sassanian.— . . well upholds joy among the people of the earth.

It will be noticed that there is an addition in this line to the previous formula, in the introduction of two new words, which are expressed in mere letters as היף and ايو respectively, to which I myself have but cautiously, and, at last, of very necessity, admitted a perhaps over simple meaning.

[1] Arabic lexicographers bring the whole series of parallel terms for Prophet under the common root نَبَا.

But having reached thus much of the conventionality of the then local speech, so marked *in situ*, and so singularly preserved in the dependent ramifications of the more advanced vernacular in its ultimate spread, I feel that but few will be found to contest the data the rock records of the middle of the third century A.D. so strangely reproduce as specimens of the crude prayers and invocations of a new faith, neither the matter nor manner of which was fully understood by the compiler of the inscription.

But of all the quaint problems that have presented themselves during the course of this rather tedious development of a complicated and obscure bilingual manifesto, no single item has afforded so much of a surprise as this *Hip* of the Chaldæan texts, which even the most daring ingenuity would scarcely have ventured to coerce into the modern Persian conversational and sonorously aspirated خوب *Khúb*,[1] unless the fellow version had contributed both the first hint and the simultaneous proof of the correctness of the assignment; even now, many critics may refuse to see the Greek εὖ in the ايو of the Sassanian writing, especially as the meaning, in either case, so oddly accords with the general tendency of the translation which I may be supposed to be too hastily advocating.

ו הדיא כלהו שיתי היף שרי

و هتيا ولزكث چيتاني ايو شديتن

C. Pehlvi.—And THE God he (is), Lord, great in goodness.

Sassanian.—And THE God that (is), Godlike, abounding in goodness.

ו מנו הדיא כלהו שיתי יאמוד להוף ידא רוב הדין

اهرمنو چتيا ولزكث چيتان رميتن ولي ليدي نب

C. Pehlvi.—And THE heavenly Lord he (is) Lord; Oh increase of good aid, Lord of Lords.

Sassanian.—And THE heavenly Lord, that (is) Lord on high, Master (giver) of aid, Lord!

[1] The orthography, in this instance, may have been affected by the Arabic هوب pro هيب, "Formidabilis, and verendus, reverendus, fuit." The Persian word is more correctly defined in line fourteen of the original inscription as חוף = هوب.

But little remains to be said in the way of strictly philological commentary upon the concluding passages of the parallel inscriptions, though their curt and imperfectly connected sentences necessarily admit of many and obvious gradational renderings. However, as any possible divarication from the leading intention of these epigraphs must, after all, revert to the general tenets of the Christian faith, we have only to accept this singular Eastern paraphrase of portions of our own authorised version, and, under such a concession, frankly to test and compare its very limited departure either in words or ideas from the Greek of the New Testament, on which we base our own interpretation.

The first of the remaining difficulties consists of a question of grammar, which was at this time, necessarily, but little subject to fixed laws; and even had the parts of speech been in any way reduced to a recognised and defined system, the eccentric intermixture of words, phrases, and constructive identities of this Camp language,[1] would release a modern interpreter from any reserve in dealing with doubtful or exceptional terms of minor significance.

[1] The direct effect of Sapur's campaigns to the westward upon the Court language of Persia has been for long past fully recognised and understood (Mohl, Preface to Shâh Nâmah), but we could scarcely have anticipated its resulting in so incoherent a polyglot as these Bilingual texts present us with. It is true that Persepolis was peculiarly situated in regard to conterminous languages, both old and new, and Sapor's freshly imported Aramaisms may have added to the normal difficulties; but much of the imperfection of these writings is undoubtedly due to the novelty of the subject, and to the impossibility of rendering whatever may have been the peculiar form of the recognised sacred text, into degraded Persian *vernaculars*, with even a remote chance of its essential meaning ultimately reaching the understanding of the less educated masses. And this, indeed, is the fatal obstacle to all Christian teaching in India at the present day,—not that we English are unfaithful, or unwilling, but that Eastern and Western thoughts and deductions start from different bases of symbolical ideals. Though the whole question only amounts to this, after all, that our Western instruction in Christianity commenced later in the world's history, and under the influence of comparatively advanced knowledge and more or less purified teaching. Europe at large received the Gospel in its best form, but every step it went Eastward, it had from the first to encounter hostilities and to submit to concessions of a character calculated to degrade its sublimity,—it was, in effect, the going back to old and self-willed races, instead of carrying welcome tidings to simple but intelligent, though undeveloped peoples.

Under the most simple and ordinary processes of critical analysis of an epigraph freely abounding in both Hebrew and Arabic terms, it might almost be taken for granted that the word כל, in lines twelve and thirteen, merely reproduced the established כֹּל, كُلّ, "all," of the authorized speech of those confessedly leading Semitic authorities; and though, with some straining, it might be possible to connect the word, in a vague way, with a suggestion of "universality," it is far preferable to let it down into the quietude of its more direct associations, and to suppose that כל is nothing more than a local reflex of the Arabic article ال, "the." It is quite true that in this very version the corresponding Hebrew ה (for הל) has been recognised in its proper and correct form; but in so strangely composite a manifesto as the present, simplicity, or a reduction to primitive elements, is the only true safeguard towards ultimate elucidation; and as we know, on the other hand, that the Persian tongue was then (as it is now) altogether deficient in any representative of our ever-recurring definite article "*the*," which, in these combinations of languages, it had to borrow with more or less *sonal* aptitude from neighbouring nations; can it then be felt strange that the severe "*lâm, of definition*," with its prosthetic ا, at this time only colloquially developed, should have been so readily merged into the Sassanian ول or the but faintly removed Chaldæan כל now under discussion.

The leading derivation and ample duties of زَكْ have already been referred to (p. 42), and the הו=هُوَ, "he," of the associate text, scarcely admits of doubt.

The single word that still remains to be noticed is the אי מזוד, which seems to resolve itself into the Arabic interjection يا (Persian اي) "oh," prefixed to the word مَزِيدٌ (here written مزود), "increase, addition," etc. (from زَادَ, "increvit"). This combination may appear strange and the exclamation somewhat out of place; but in regard to مزيد, it must be remembered how constantly the exact synonym افزود, "increase," was in use,—to such an extent, indeed, that the Pehlvi

افزوت = یوسکوام came to hold the place of honour on the obverse field of the later Sassanian coins, and was retained intact by the Arabs in their imitative coinage, and only disappeared with the latest Pehlvi mintages of Taberistán in A.H. 138.[1]

PARALLEL TRANSLATIONS OF THE HAJIÁBÁD INSCRIPTION.

(For text see page 74 and the Photograph.)

CHALDÆO-PEHLVI VERSION: Representations of the person of the
SASSANIAN VERSION: *Representations of the person of the Zoro-*
Zoroastrian divinity,[2] Sapor, King of Kings of Arians and Anarians,
astrian divinity, Sapor, King of Kings of Irán and Anirán, of
of divine origin from God, son of the Zoroastrian divinity, Ardeshír,
divine origin from God, son of the Zoroastrian divinity, Artahshatr,
King of Kings of Arians, of divine origin from God, grandson of divine
King of Kings of Irán, of divine origin from God, grandson of divine
Papak, King. And of multitudes of men, Lord, mighty, the
Papak, King. Also Lord of many races, sole mighty (one) of the high
obeyed of Satraps, Military chiefs, Nobles. And YE mighty
Satraps, and Military commanders, and Nobles. And YE mighty
(one) and bringer of joy among the people of the world, and God of
(one) also bringing joy (salvation?) to the people of earth, also God of
Justice he (is), Lord of the Creator, the high Creator, the Seed (of)
Might he (is), Lord of the Creator, the heavenly Creator, the Vicar of
the FIRST of Gods, the Spirit he (is). . . . . . over the Jews sole
the high God of Gods, the Seed. And Lord who of the Archon of the
Lord created YE (are). . . . . . . of the order of the chosen Jews
Jews sole Lord of Lords he (is). Supreme Lord of the Jews "without

[1] J.R.A.S. xii. 347. In the higher sense see St. Luke xvii. 5, Πρόσθες ἡμῖν πίστιν, "Increase our faith." Acts vi. 7, Καὶ ὁ λόγος τοῦ Θεοῦ ηὔξανε, "and the word of God increased." 1 Corinthians iii. 6, ἀλλ' ὁ Θεὸς ηὔξανεν, "but God gave the increase." 7. ἀλλ' ὁ αὐξάνων Θεός, "but God gave the increase." 2 Cor. x. 15; Ephesians iv. 16; Col. i. 10; ii. 19, αὔξει τὴν αὔξησιν τοῦ Θεοῦ, "increaseth with the increase of God." 1 Thess. iii. 12; iv. 10, etc.

[2] It will be seen that I have varied many of the details which were more severely treated in the preceding commentary, among the rest I have altered the rendering of the word مزدیسن. If the term "*Mazdyasna* religion" has been correctly assigned to the creed itself, it will be quite optional to convert the "Ormazd-worshipper" of the present text into the "Zoroastrian."

ye (are). Of a certainty the Master, the Divine Lord [first in rank]
the law" he (is). And, of a certainty, the Master, Heavenly Lord (first
created Jesus of divine aid THE Lord thou (art) bringing mercifully
in order) Lord . . . . of divine aid he, who well brings joy
joy to the people of the world. And THE GOD he (is) Lord, abound-
among the people of the earth. And THE God, that is Godlike, great
ing in good. And THE Heavenly Lord he (is) Lord, oh Increase
in goodness. And the heavenly Lord that (is) Lord on high, master
of good aid, Lord of Lords.
of aid Lord.

Such, then, is my first attempt at anything like an intelligible translation of this obscure inscription. I can hardly say that I am altogether satisfied with the result, which has proved as unexpected to myself as it may chance to seem incredible to others; but my convictions have merely followed a confessedly tentative lead, and many things that I was prepared to discredit in the preliminary investigation, have, in the progress of more exact examination, contributed the best support towards a consistent whole. As far as honest criticism extends, I court and desire it; but I would suggest to those who may propose to make capital for themselves out of my treatment of this record, to beware of the many pitfalls existing in so incoherent and singularly mixed a text, the limited extent of which forbids the application of any such comprehensive tests as its confessedly polyglot nature would demand; and in this sense I do not invite future commentators to wander over other applicable roots, or to suggest variations in the derivatives above cited; but I simply ask them to produce some more consistent and convincing version out of the given fourteen lines here reconstructed from the confessedly imperfect materials at present within reach.[1]

It is of importance to fix as nearly as possible the period of

[1] It may, perhaps, prove an inducement and an encouragement to those who might otherwise feel diffident in entering upon a free and independent analysis of future improved versions of the leading texts—to learn that Sir H. Rawlinson altogether dissents from and contests the fundamental principles of the present avowedly suggestive translation.

Sapor's reign, to which this unique manifesto refers. I have already remarked (pp. 88, 97) upon the change in style and modification of certain expressions to be observed in the concluding part of the document; but further than this, a close examination of the original writing discloses, most distinctly, a parallel variation in the general run of the letters themselves; for, whereas, the first five lines of the Chaldæo-Pehlvi text[1] are, so to say, compact in the ordinary sequence of the characters, the remaining portion, and notably, the conclusion of the inscription, is not only less closely filled in, but the words are designedly and effectively separated from one another,—a condition of things that would imply not only that the original surface of the rock had been prepared for a longer legend than it now bears, but that the commencement and conclusion of the existing epigraph pertain to different epochs, even as their tenor, at first sight, seems inconsistent and conflicting within such brief limits; but, singular to say, these apparent anomalies conduce to a most reasonable explanation of what would otherwise undoubtedly have constituted a serious difficulty in the completeness of the proposed interpretation. As it is, I suppose the introductory section, containing the formal enumeration of the King's titles and descent, with his claims to divine honors, extending, *inter alia*, to a subdued profession of Zoroastrianism itself, to have been endorsed at some early period of his reign, after he had discarded the use of the Greek translations, in the addition of which he had at first followed his father's lead (Inscrip. No. IV.); but before he had altogether abandoned the employment of the accustomed Chaldæo-Pehlvi duplicate version, and confined himself to the use of simple Persian-Pehlvi, which survived as the sole Court and official method of epigraphy among his successors. Under such a theory, I should associate the abrupt change in the tenor of the body of the document with the Western influences to which Sapor was subjected after his conquest of Valerian, a period which oddly coincides with the commencement of the teaching of Manes

[1] The sixth line of the Sassanian Pehlvi likewise presents a perceptible but less obvious modification of the forms of letters employed in the opening sentence.

(A.D. 261).[1] It is possible that this individual, who—though born a Persian—had graduated as a Christian Presbyter in Babylonia, may have been the direct means of converting the victorious monarch of his own land to the true faith; while the disruption of the association and the precipitate flight of Manes from Persia may have been due to a premature attempt on his part to compromise his Sovereign by lowering Christianity to the dead level of the masses, or by too facile concessions to the dominant Zoroastrianism, but lately so powerfully reconstructed under Ardeshir Babagán. However, be this as it may, it is clear that Sapor was an oddly-confessed convert,—no subject, high or low, under an Eastern despotism, would have dared to add such sentences as are to be found in this inscription without the sanction of the reigning Monarch; nor can we suppose that if Sapor had ever reverted to the newly defined creed of his fathers, he would have allowed this formal record of his adhesion to a more enlightened religion to have remained undisturbed till his death. The return of Manes after the decease of Sapor, and the favour with which he was received by Hormuzdas I., are both significant; for, if the new king had been a confirmed Fire-worshipper, he would scarcely have tolerated even the scant measure of debased Christianity Manes to the last professed to expound.

[1] It has for long past been known and acknowledged that Sapor had abandoned the creed of his fathers, though it was supposed that he had accepted the tenets of Manes. The following is Masudi's notice on the subject:—"Ce fut sous son règne que parut Manès, l'auteur du dualisme. Sabour abjura la religion des mages pour embrasser cette secte et les doctrines qu'elle professait sur la lumière et le moyen de combattre le principe des ténèbres; mais il revint plus tard au culte de ses ancêtres, et Manès, pour des motifs que nous avons rapportés dans nos récits précédents, dut se réfugier dans l'Inde."—Masudi, cap. xxiv. vol. ii., p. 164, Paris edit.—"C'est du vivant de Manès que fut créé le mot *zendik*, qui a donné naissance au *zendekeh* (manichéisme). En voici l'explication: Zeradecht fils d'Espiman, . . . avait apporté aux Perses le livre *Bestah*, rédigé dans leur ancienne langue. Il en donna un commentaire qui est le *Zend*, et il ajouta ensuite à ce commentaire une glose qu'il nomma *Bazend*. Ainsi, le Zend contenait l'explication du premier livre révélé. Plus tard, tous ceux qui, dans cette religion, s'écartèrent du *Bestah* ou livre révélé, pour se conformer au Zend, c'est-à-dire au commentaire, furent appelés *Zendi*, du nom de ce commentaire; ce qui signifiait qu'ils s'éloignaient de la lettre même du texte révélé pour adopter le sens du commentaire, par opposition avec ce texte. . . . . Le mot *zendik* désigna alors les dualistes et tous ceux qui professaient la croyance en l'éternité du monde et niaient la création."—Masudi, cap xxiv.—Further notices of Manes and his doctrines are to be found in Hamza Isfahâni, p. 36; Abulfaraj (Pocock) pp. 82, 83; Tabari, Persian MS., details given under the reign of Bahrâm; Histoire Critique de Manichée, M. de Beausobre, Amsterdam, 1734, pp. l. 24, 66, 81, 83, 156–161, 167, 192, etc.; Clinton, Fasti Romani, ii. p. 424.; Mani. Gustav Flügel, Leipzig, 1862.

Inscription No. 7. (Narses.)

This unique inscription of Narses is engraved on one of the bas-reliefs[1] at Sháhpúr, which represents the young monarch in the act of receiving the conventional investiture of the cydaris from Ormazd. The figure of the latter is but little varied from the ordinary portraiture of prior date. He wears the recognised mural crown, with the closely twisted curls rising above it, and similar curls, arranged in the Sassanian fashion, appear on the sides and back of the head. The beard is squared in the ancient style, and the flowing fillets expand at the back of the figure. He has, however, in this instance, no baton, and the folds of the dress have more of a feminine guise than usual. Narses appears as a fair and comely youth, with a light moustache and incipient beard, which, however, is tied determinedly towards the point, after the manner affected by Sapor I. The hair is curled in full and smooth ringlets. His dress, like that of Ormazd, and the trappings of both horses, are unusually plain. He wears a pointedly-spiked crown of a form not yet met with in the sculptures, but which is seen to have been previously in use with Varahran I. on the coinage of the country.[2] The authorized balloon-crest and floating fillets complete the picture.

This inscription was first published by Morier, in his work upon Persia, Armenia, etc.,[3] but the copy there given is truncated in the completion of the lines, two of which (Nos. nine and ten) are wholly omitted, and the letters are so badly formed that it offered but little promise to the decipherer. M. Flandin's reproduction of the original is far more satisfactory, and leaves but little to be filled in by a fairly confident interpreter.

It will be seen that in the inscription Narses describes himself as the son of Sapor and grandson of Ardeshir, whereas

[1] Flandin, "Inscription du troisième bas-relief sur la rive droite de la rivière." *Plan*, plate 45, bas-relief E. *Sculpture*, bas-relief E, plate 52. Text, vol. ii. p. 270. Dans le coin, à droite, au-dessus du manteau du cavalier, est une inscription en charactères Pehlvi. C'est le seule que l'on trouve à Châpour."

[2] Narses himself is figured with a totally different crown on his coinage. Longpérier, v. 2.

[3] 1812, plate xxix p. 87 and 357.

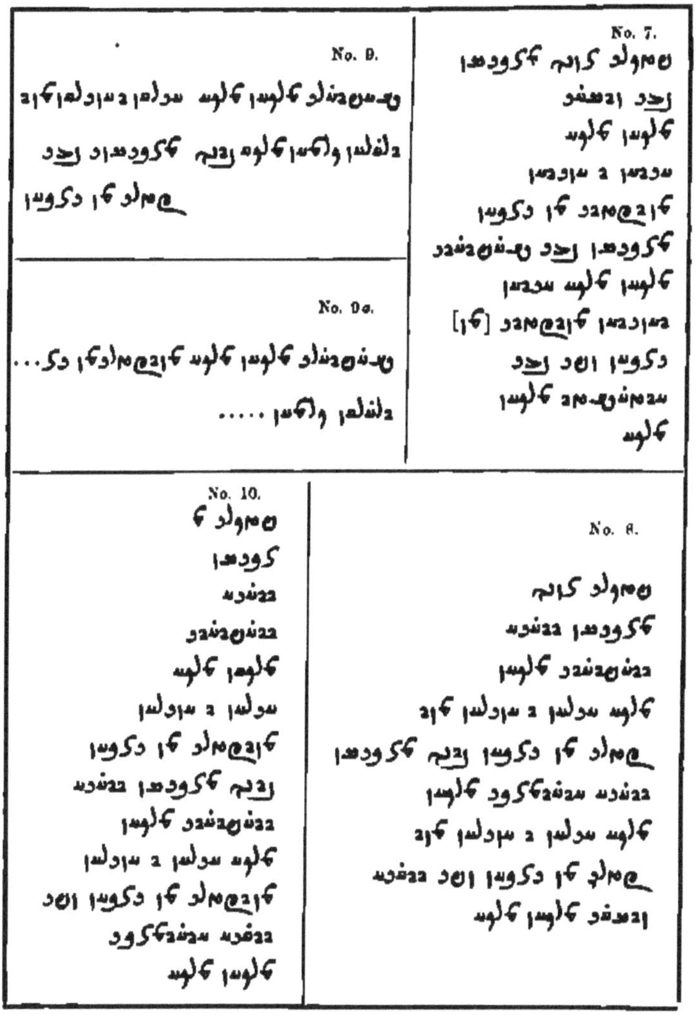
No. 7.
No. 9.
No. 9a.
No. 10.
No. 8.

he is ordinarily held to have been the son of Varahran II.[1] It is true that this may possibly have been a mere figure of speech on his part, in desiring to ignore the intermediate successions of less renowned monarchs; but there is nothing inconsistent in the youthful appearance of Narses in this sculpture with the probability of his having been, in effect, the son of the later days of Sapor, who died only some twenty-one years previous to the regal accession symbolized in the bas-relief; and, singular to say, one of the Armenian authorities lately collected by M. Evariste Prud'homme, in illustration of Sassanian history,[2] directly declares that Narses was the son of Sapor I.[3]

Inscription No. 7.—Narses, a.d. 294–303, at Shâhpûr.

II. 1 پتکري زنيِ مزديسن 2 بگي نرسهي 3 ملکان ملکا 4 ايران و انيران
5 منوچتري من يزدان [بريِ] 6 مزديسن بگي شهپوهري 7 ملکان ملکا
ايران 8 وانيران منو چتري من 9 يزدان نپي بگي 10 ارتهشتر ملکان
11 ملکا

Image of the person of Ormazd-worshipper, divine Narses, king of kings of Irán and Anirán, of heavenly origin from God, the son of Ormazd-worshipper, divine Shâhpûr, king of kings of Irán and Anirán, of heavenly origin from God, grandson of divine Artahshatr, king of kings.

Inscriptions Nos. 8 and 10.

(*Pahlvi transcript, page* 103.)

The Ṭák-i-Bustán inscriptions, identificatory of the figures of the two Sapors, the second and third of the name, sculptured under the smaller arch of the excavations in that locality, have for long past been before the public in the decipherments of De Sacy and his commentators;[4] and their final determination may now be said to be set at rest by the exact copies of Sir H. Rawlinson, here reproduced in modern characters. Unlike his previous facsimiles, which were to a certain extent

[1] Moudjmel Altawârîkh (*Journal Asiatique*, 1839, p. 38); Hamza Isfahâni, p. 37; Mirkhond, De Sacy, p. 301.
[2] *Journal Asiatique*, 1866, p. 101–238. [3] Ibid., Sépêos, p. 17.
[4] De Sacy, Mémoires sur div. Ant. p. 211, and second memoir, Journal of the Institute, 1809, vol. ii. p. 162; Ker Porter, ii. 188; Malcolm's Persia, i. 258; M. Boré, Journal Asiatique, June, 1841; M. Louis Dubeux, Journal Asiatique, 1843; Spiegel, Grammatik der Huzvareschsprache, 1856, p. 173.

mere unaided tracings, in this instance the transcriber knew both the letters and general import of the record he was employed upon, and hence his text may be freely accepted as disposing of all exceptional variants and doubtful readings. By a critical examination of these writings, Sir Henry has been enabled to rectify the constituents of the much-canvassed "*Vohiya*" of previous translators, and to establish the true value of the word, in the more natural شهيا, a correction of considerable importance, in that, while demonstrating the authorized provincial or epochally progressive substitution of two נ's for the legitimate archaic form of ש *sh*, and thus adding to the general ambiguity of Pehlvi interpretation on the one hand, it extends a new latitude to the optional reconstruction of many obscure passages, which had hitherto been circumscribed by the already sufficiently dubious phonetic powers of the leading basis here duplicated נ, which, under ordinary circumstances, had to respond alike for the powers of ر *r* and و *w*, and to meet the manifest incertitudes involved in the technical licence of subordinate convertibilities.

These lapidary epigraphs have also proved of service in contributing a modified form of the ordinary ∽ *ch*, in the shape of ∾, a contour of the letter frequently met with on gems, and which was otherwise liable to be mistaken for a simple ∽ *h*. The intentionally *final* i's are also very carefully defined, in marked contrast to the ordinary initial and medial vowel, a practice which is also scrupulously observed in the majority of the signet legends.

The statues of the two Sapors, father and son, in this bas-relief, are strangely alike, a similarity extending even to the minor details of their garments. In Ker Porter's copy, the father, who stands to the right, seems to be the larger man; but the difference in Flandin's sketch is not so apparent. The former author represents the faces of both kings as having been completely destroyed; but Flandin, having possibly cleaned the surface of the stone more effectually, reconstructs their features after the ordinary Sassanian physiognomy, with the curiously tied beards and bushy hair. Both monarchs stand to the front, with their hands crossed on the hilts of their straight swords, and the only difference to be detected between them is the half-moon which, in Flandin's drawing, figures as a frontlet on the crown of Sapor III.

The sculptured effigies of the two kings in their near identity of treatment would seem to imply that they must have been executed almost simultaneously, and the juxtaposition itself may possibly have been designed to mark in one and the same field the father's recognition of the heirship of this particular son, who eventually succeeded to his throne in the ordinary course.

Inscription No. 8.—Sháhpúr II. A.D. 310–381, at Ták-i-Bustán.

[1] پتکري [2] زني مزديسن شهيا [3] شبپوهري ملکان [4] ملکا ايران و
انيران منو [5] چتري من يزدان بري مزديسن [6] شهيا اوهرمزدي ملکان
[7] ملکا ايران و انيران منو [8] چتري من يزدان نبي شهيا [9] نرسهي
ملکان ملکا

Inscription No. 10.—Sháhpúr III., son of Sháhpúr, A.D. 385–390, at Ták-i-Bustán.

[1] پتکري [2] زني مزديسن [3] شهيا [4] شهپوهري [5] ملکان ملکا [6] ايران و
انيران [7] منو چتري من يزدان [8] بري مزديسن شهيا [9] شهپوهري ملکان
[10] ملکا ايران و انيران [11] منو چتري من يزدان نبي [12] شهيا اوهرمزدي
[13] ملکان ملکا

Inscription No. 9.

The intervening legends in this series have been recovered from another class of dynastic remains, being taken from the still extant official signets of Varahrán Kermán Sháh, the son of the great Sapor *Zu'laktaf*, under whom he administered the important government from which his title was derived. In a section of the old world, where the seal so readily adapted itself to the indigenous clay,[1] and where all

[1] Job xxxviii. 14. See also Gen. xxxviii. 18, 25; xli. 42; Exod. xxviii. 9, 10, 11, 21, 36; 1 Kings xxi. 8; Neh. ix. 38; Esth. iii. 10, 12; viii. 2, 8, 10; Song of Solomon viii. 6; Jerem. xxxii. 10, 12, 44; Dan. vi. 17; Matt. xxvii. 66.

men carried seals;[1] indeed, where everything was sealed, from the formal documents on terra cotta and other substances, down to the mouth of the lion's den and the stone of the sepulchre, it was natural that the Signets of Kings should typify a parallel ascendancy,[2] and as such carry a political import equal, if not superior, to that of the Crown itself.[3] As this same section of the earth's surface passed under the subjection of dynasty after dynasty, ancient ideas still held their sway, and in the advance of civilization as types and devices were elaborated among the masses, the representatives of the Royal sign manual were naturally more carefully treated, and at last, under the Sassanians, the complications of Persian ceremonial had arrived at a subdivision involving

[1] Herodotus, i. 195; iii. 128; vii. 69; Strabo, xvi. c. i. § 20; Ctesias (Phot.) lvii. 2, 5; Xenophon Cyrop. viii. c. 2, § 16, 17.

[2] A striking instance of the importance attached to Royal Signets, in very early times, has lately been contributed by Sir H. Rawlinson's decipherments of Cuneiform documents. Sir H. remarks: "I have recently lighted on a small clay tablet at the British Museum which bears an inscription to the following effect:—

"*Tiglath-Usur*, king of Assyria, son of *Shalman-Usur*, king of Assyria, and conqueror of *Kar-Duniš* (Babylonia). Whoever injures my device (?) or name, may *Asshur* and *Yama* destroy his name and country."

"A signet-seal with this legend having been carried off as a trophy in war from Assyria to Babylon, I, Sennacherib, king of Assyria, after 600 years, took the city of Babylon, and from among the spoils of Babylon recovered it."

"The reverse of the tablet contains a repetition of the legend of *Tiglath-Usur* with the gloss, 'This is what was written on the signet-seal.'"
—*Athenæum*, 22nd August, 1863.

[3] Alexander "Literas quoque, quas in Europam mitteret, veteris annuli gemma obsignabat; iis, quas in Asiam scriberet, Darii annulus imprimebatur."—Quintus Curtius, vi. c. 6, § 6. See also x. vi. 4: "Tunc Perdiccas, regia sella in conspectum vulgi data, in qua diadema vestisque Alexandri cum armis erant, annulum sibi pridie traditum a rege in eadem sede posuit." 5. "Et Perdiccas, Ego quidem, inquit, annulum, quo ille regni atque imperii vires obsignare erat solitus, traditum ab ipso mihi, reddo vobis." See also Josephus Ant. xii. c. 9, § 2; xx. c. 2, § 3. So also Justin. "Sexta die praeclusa voce exemptum digito annulum Perdiccae tradidit. Nam etsi non voce nuncupatus heres, judicio tamen electus videbatur." xii. c. 15, § 12.

In like manner Pompey's "Head and Seal" are brought to Julius Cæsar. Plutarch, in Pompey lxxx. and in Cæsar xlviii. Dion Cassius, xlii. 7, *μέχρις οὗ τήν τε κεφαλὴν καὶ τὸν δακτύλιον αὐτοῦ πεμφθέντα οἱ ὑπὸ τοῦ Πτολεμαίου εἶδεν.* Dion Cass. xlii. 18, *ἐπεὶ μέντοι καὶ ἐνέθανεν, ἐφ' ὃ μὲν καὶ τοῦτο, καὶ οὐ πρότερον, πρὶν τὸν δακτύλιον αὐτοῦ πεμφθέντα ἰδεῖν, ἐπίστευσαν· ἐνεγέγλυπτο δὲ ἐν αὐτῷ τρόπαια τρία, ὥσπερ καὶ ἐν τῷ τοῦ Σύλλου.*

a separate seal and distinct device for every one of the nine departments of the State administration.[1]

In Egypt and to the westward men's signets were set in the form of finger rings, but in the East, among the lightly-

[1] Ce roi [Naushirwán] employait quatre sceaux d'État. Celui de l'impôt . . avait pour empreinte la Justice (العدل). Le sceau des domaines, orné d'une turquoise, avait pour empreinte l'Agriculture (العمارة). Le sceau du conseil avait un rubis (*Kuhli* كحلى) et portait l'empreinte de la Temporisation (التانى) Le sceau des postes . . . avait pour empreinte la Fidélité (الوفاء).—Mas'udi, ii. 204.

Khusru Parviz had nine different State seals. Mas'udi gives the following details regarding their forms and uses. Le premier était un anneau (خاتم) de diamant dont le chaton était formé d'un rubis rouge sur lequel on avait gravé le portrait du roi; la légende portait les titres du roi; on l'apposait sur les lettres et les diplômes. Le second était un anneau (خاتم) d'or surmonté d'une cornaline sur laquelle étaient gravés les mots Khoraçân Khudah (خراسان خده). Il servait aux archives de l'État. Le troisième était orné d'un onyx représentant un cavalier au galop; l'anneau (حلقة), qui était d'or, portait pour légende: *célérité*. Ce cachet était destiné à la correspondance des postes. Le quatrième était un anneau d'or dont le chaton, formé d'un rubis rose, avait pour légende: la richesse est la source de la prospérité. C'était le sceau des diplômes et des lettres de grâce. Le cinquième, orné d'un rubis *bahrmân*, . . . portait les mots khourah wa khorrem (خره و خرم) "splendeur et félicité." Ce cachet était posé sur le trésor des pierres précieuses sur la cassette royale, la garde-robe et les ornements de la couronne. Le sixième, représentant un aigle, servait à sceller les dépêches adressés aux rois étrangers; son chaton était en fer de Chine (حديد صينى). Le septième, surmonté d'un bésoard sur lequel on avait gravé une mouche, était posé sur les mets servis au roi, sur les médicaments et les parfums. Le huitième, dont le chaton était formé d'une perle, avait pour effigie une tête de porc (Journal Asiatique, 1863, p. 304); on posait cette empreinte sur le cou des condamnés à mort et sur les arrêts emportant la peine capitale. Le neuvième était un anneau de fer que le roi employait quand il allait au bain et dans les étuves." ii. 228-9.

The latest development of the art of sealing is highly amusing. We learn from Captain Montgomerie's report of the great Tibetan road from Lhasa to Gartokh (*Times*, 2nd March, 1868) "that the couriers go continuously, stopping neither night nor day except to eat and change horses, and, after an 800 miles' ride, are haggard and worn . . . . to make sure that they shall not take off their clothes they are sealed over the breast, and none may break the seal save him to whom the messenger is sent."

For confirmation of these facts, see also the "Friend of India" (Calcutta), 23rd March, 1868. "The moment a man is selected as a courier, and his coat is sealed, he has no choice in the matter."

clad multitudes, they were simply suspended round the neck, while the better classes seem to have worn them either on the wrist or as an armlet.[1]

The first of these seals is engraved on the highly-prized amethyst belonging to the Duke of Devonshire. The second is now known only by its reproduction in a work of the last century, entitled "Tassie's Gems." It would seem to have proved from the first a mere artist's failure both in the portrait and in the imperfection of the legend, and to have been superseded by the more elaborately engraved design, giving the accepted likeness of the Prince, with his style and contrasted royal titles encompassing it in the Pehlvi character. The portrait, in this instance, presents a remarkable specimen

[1] This arrangement is shown to have been in immemorial acceptation in the far East, by numerous passages in the Shâh Nâmah; among the rest, when Rustam takes leave of his wife *Tahmimah*, the daughter of the king of Samangân, we are told

ببازوي رستم يكي مهره بود   كه آن مهره اندر جهان شهره بود

بدو داد وگفتش كه اين‌را بدار   گرت دختري آيد از روزگار

بگير و بگيسوي او بر بدوز   بنيك اختر و فال گيتي فروز

ور ايدون كه آيد ز اختر پسر   ببندش ببازو بسان پدر

Mohl. Paris edition, ii., p. 81. Macan. i. p. 336.

The conclusion of this passage has been quaintly paraphrased by an early English translator in the following couplets:—

"This seal with care preserve, and if by Heaven
To your caress a daughter may be given,
Upon her hair you must this charm entwine
As an auspicious star and happy sign.
But if a son be born, his arm around
Let this insignium of his sire be bound."

—C. T. Robertson, Calcutta, 1829, p. 18.

So also, in the fatal single combat between father and son, in front of the hostile hosts of Irán and Turán, whose several nationalities each is supposed to represent—where the son fights with the full knowledge of the person of his adversary, but Rustam is ignorant that Sohráb is the offspring of his own deserted wife,—the latter in his dying moments reveals himself with the expression, "Thy seal upon my arm behold." (ببازوم بر مهرهٔ خود نگر)

of Oriental youthful beauty, of which I have vainly sought to obtain a thoroughly satisfactory representation, though the accompanying woodcut gives a very artistic rendering

Head of Varahrán, from the Devonshire Amethyst.

(*True size of the seal,* 1·25 × 1·05 *inches.*)

of the general details. The following is a fac-simile of the legend that surrounds the bust on the signet:[1]—

Inscription No. 9.—Varahrán, Kirmán Sháh, seal in use during the lifetime of his Father, Sapor II., Zu'laktaf.

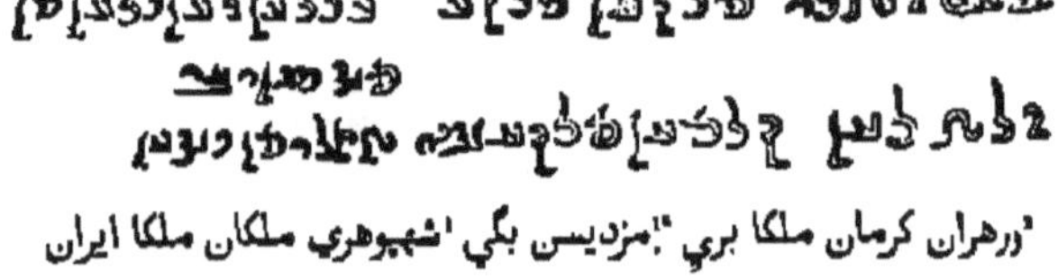

ورهران كرمان ملكا بري مزديسن بگي شهپوهري ملكان ملكا ايران

و انيران منو چتري من يزدان

Varahrán, king of Kermán, the son of Ormazd-worshipper, divine Shahpúr, king of kings of Irán and Anirán, of celestial origin from God.

[1] *Numismatic Chronicle*, N. S. vol. vi. p. 241.

The second less perfect seal, to judge from the engraving of 1791,[1] does a certain amount of justice to the profile of the Prince, who is there figured with a full and well arranged beard and curled locks, while his Parthian helmet is adorned with the self-same device as is seen on the more valuable gem. The inscription, however, breaks off abruptly, though the introductory portion follows the arrangement of the lines of the legend above given, while the منوچتري which follows *in line* after the ملکا, and the reduced size of the letters of the name of *Varahrán*, sufficiently establish that the first published design is not a mere vague copy of the more finished seal. The transcript in modern Persian runs—

شهپوهري ملکان ملکا منوچتري من يز . . .

ورهران کرمان . .

It seems, it must be confessed, a strange hazard that brings to us, from a far distant land, two if not three signets of a king who lived nearly fifteen centuries ago.

The authenticity of the portrait-seal of Varahrán, employed while he was his father's viceroy, in *Kermán*, is sufficiently attested by the legends on its surface. The signet we have now to deal with as clearly declares its associations, though in a less formal manner, inasmuch as the style of head-dress borne by the chief figure typifies the conventionally distinguishing crown of Varahrán IV. as "king of kings," or after his accession to Imperial honors.[2]

The seals of the deceased Sassanian princes were, without doubt, religiously preserved in the Jewel Treasuries of the family, who, as we have seen, were sufficiently jealous and punctilious in these matters; so that nothing short of a total disruption of dynastic ties would be likely to have scattered abroad such cherished symbols of ancestral domination; but precisely such an extreme convulsion took place some 250 years

[1] Tassie's Gems (London, 1791), pl. xii. fig. 673, vol. I. p. 66. See also Ouseley's "Medals and Gems" (London, 1801).

[2] The date of this event is not very exactly determined, but it may be placed in 389 A.D., with a reign of ten years, extending to 399 A.D. Clinton, from Western sources, fixes his advent to the throne in 388 A.D.—Fasti Romani, p. 518.

later, in the total conquest of Persia by the early Muhammadan Arabs, whose practice of dividing the spoil, on the one part,[1] and their objection, then but partially developed, to graven images, on the other, would equally conduce to the dispersion of the more or less correctly-appreciated valuables of this description.[2]

The gem in question, an engraving of which is given in the margin, has lately been brought to this country by General A. Cunningham, to whom I am indebted for my present knowledge of it, as well as for many recent obligations of the same nature.

The seal is sunk into a dark onyx, upon whose upper surface a milk-white film has been allowed to remain. It is stated to have been obtained from Ráwal Pindi, in the Punjáb.

On the first cursory inspection of the device, a suggestion arose as to whether the standing figure might not represent the oft-recurring Sapor I. with the prostrate Valerian at his feet? But it was felt that, as a general rule, the coin portraiture of each Sassanian king had been intentionally reduced to a definite typical model in respect to the form of the crown,—which suffices, even in these days, to determine, with almost invariable precision, the individual monarch to whom any given piece should be assigned, however obscure or defaced the descriptive legends may chance to be.

Ardeshir Babegán, and more notably Sapor I., as we have seen, varied with the progress of their arms the forms and representative devices of their crowns; but their successors

[1] After the battle of Kadesia, the spoils, after deducting one-fifth for the Khalif, were divided among the sixty thousand horsemen at the estimated rate of 12,000 dínárs each!—Price, Muhammadan Hist. i. 117, 120, 121.

[2] There are odd tales, alike, of the Conquerors, from the desert, offering gold for the better-known silver, and of their being unable to distinguish camphor from salt, etc.; but in regard to the number of precious stones stored up and partially adapted to the purposes of Oriental display, there can be no question. The carpet of "Cloth of Gold," of 60 cubits square, had its pattern fashioned of jewels of the highest value. This was cut up into small pieces, "one of which, of the size only of the palm of a man's hand," was afterwards sold for 20,000 dirhams; or, as others say, for the same number of dínárs."—See Price, 117, 121, 122, etc.

necessarily exercised less licence in this respect, though the sculptured representations were not always bound by Mint laws. The first monarch who adopted, on the public money, the design of head-dress introduced by Sapor I. (as figured in page 62), was Varahrán II., at least to this particular one of the several kings of the name are all coins distinguished by this style of head-gear, by common consent, attributed; and to Varahrán IV. are assigned, by the equally arbitrary decisions of Numismatists, all those pieces that are marked by the subsidiary modification upon the earlier form, comprised in the introduction of the projecting front of the mural crown, in advance of the established eagle's wings; and it is this peculiarity alone that, in the present state of our knowledge, determines the attribution of the seal to the last-named ruler.[1]

The subordinate prostrate figure is evidently designed to represent a Roman warrior, but the semblance of the "laureated" Valerian of the sculptures is altogether abandoned; and though it may be freely admitted that the helmet with the flowing plume, here depicted, is identical with the design adhered to in the leading Imperial mintages of his period,[2] yet it must be remembered that there were many such western casques left behind in Persia, to serve as models for artistic

[1] Some of the local historical authors pretend to give descriptions of each Sassanian king's costume in succession, from a book of portraits, which was supposed to carry considerable authenticity. The following is Hamza's account of Varahrán the IV.'s dress and appointments:—"Vestis coerulea est, acu picta, braccæ rubræ itemque picturatæ, corona viridis inter tres apices et lunulam auream; stat, dextra manu hastam tenens, sinistra gladio innixus" (p. 39). The description of the crown in the original text is couched in the following terms:— و تاجه اخضر بين ثلث شرفات و مازرج ذهب. The شرفات may possibly refer to the three projections of the mural crown (شُرَّافَة Pinna arcis vel muri). The Persian version in the Mujmal-al-Tawárikh has شرفه. (M. Quatremère, in the Journal Asiatique, 1839.) The مازرج has very much the air of the ordinary Persian مادرخ, which would so nearly accord with the Arabic هلال in the parallel descriptive passages.

[2] Visconti. Icon. Rom. vol. iii. pl. 56, Nos. 10 and 13. See also Trésor de Numismatique Icon. Rom. Helmet of Gallienus (pl. lii. fig. 5), and his successors.

reproductions, even if, in the interval, any general change in equipment of the Byzantine legions had been sufficiently obvious to reach Oriental perceptions. So that with the parallel divergences of forms and types, it will be preferable, under all circumstances, to assign this seal to the later epoch.

The device of an Assyrian king in the act of slaying a lion was a favourite subject for royal signets in very early times,[1] and the same symbol of power entered largely into the figurative sculptures of the Achæmenians at Persepolis; mutatis mutandis, amid the more civilized tendencies of the fourth century A.D., Varahrân reproduces a similar idea, but replaces the lion by the type of the normal national adversary. There is no record, as far as can be ascertained, of Varahrân having personally encountered the Romans after his accession,[2] but it is not impossible that he may have fleshed his maiden sword during the campaigns of his father, Sapor II., against Constantius, Julian, and Jovian, or on later chance occasions; and hence may have adopted this emblematic device on his seal, as Sulla adhered to the gem which depicted his early success against Jugurtha.[3]

I conclude this *résumé* of the extant Sassanian inscriptions by a reference to two mural epigraphs at Persepolis, copied by Sir Wm. Ouseley in 1811,[4] which, so far as I am aware, have not been reproduced by any other traveller.[5] The original writing does not seem to have afforded a very favourable text, and the coarse and straggling lithographed copy inserted in "Ouseley's Travels," is anything but encouraging

[1] Layard, Nineveh and Babylon, 154; Ker Porter, ii., pl. 64, etc.; Flandin, iii., pls. 121 *bis*, 122, 123, etc.; G. Rawlinson, Ancient Monarchies, ii. 123; iii. 338.

[2] The treaty of peace with Rome was ratified in 384 A.D.

[3] Pliny, xxxvii. 4; Plutarch in C. Marius, x; Valerius Maximus, viii. 8, xiv. § 4.

[4] In the inner chamber of the Hall of Columns at Persepolis, among the various inscriptions in other characters, "we also find two *Pahlavi* inscriptions, which, though slightly cut, are sufficiently conspicuous; yet no former traveller has, perhaps, taken the trouble of copying them. In plate xlii. both are given; one containing twelve lines, the other eleven. While copying these inscriptions from the marble, I reduced each letter to about half of the original size. They record the names and titles of Shâhpûhr, Auhormizdi, and Varahrân. Among all the ruins at *Takht-i-Jemshid*, I did not perceive any other specimen of Pahlavi writing."—Vol. ii. p. 238.

[5] Flandin adverts to them in general terms, but gives no copies.—Folio, texte, p. 1060.

to the home decipherer. I have given a few broken specimens of the more legible portions, from which it would seem that the one inscription refers to Sapor II. and the other to Sapor III. The style of the associated inscriptions varies considerably, both in words and letters. No. xi. uses the ڵ *l* in Sapor's name instead of the 2 *r*, and introduces a زي *zj*, "of," between the King's name and his titles. The word هوي occurs once if not twice in those portions of the text in which I have not as yet succeeded in tracing a running context sufficient to justify even a suggestive restoration.

It will be noticed that the genealogy of Sapor III., as given in No. xii., differs from that recorded at Ṭáḳ-i-Dustán: here he is represented as the great-grandson of Varahrán, while in the Northern inscriptions (Nos. viii. x.), where his own descent is carried up two generations, and extended in his father's official pedigree to a common ancestor, the great grandfather would appear to have been Narses. But even supposing Sir W. Ouseley has not been hasty in his decipherment of the name of Varahrán, which, however, comes out clearly enough in his facsimile, it would always be preferable to accept the more proximate and immediate declaration of lineage from Narses, and to infer that the Southern annalists of later days were careless about remote descents.

INSCRIPTION No. XI. SAPOR II. SON OF HORMAZDAS II. (Sir W. Ouseley vol. ii. pl. xliii. B.)

1 . اوهرمزدي . . . . ملكا . . .

3 شهبوهلي زي

4 ملكان ملكا

5 شهبوهلي زي ملكان ملكا ايران و انيران [منوچتر]

7 شهبوهلي زي ملكان ملكا ايران و انيران [منوچترمن]

7 [يزدان] شهبوهلي زي ملكان ملكا . . . .

8 شهبولي زي ملكان ملكا

9 شهيا

10 [شهب]وهلي زي ملكان ملكا

INSCRIPTION No. XII. SAPOR III. SON OF SAPOR II. (Sir W. Ouseley, vol ii. pl. xliii. A.)

1 . . . . مزديسن بگي شهپوهر ملكان ملكا ايران

2 وانيران منوچتري من يزدان بري مزديسن شهيا شهپوهري مكان ملكا ايران

3 وانيران منوچتري من يزدان بري مزديسن بگي اوهرمزدي ملكان ملكا ايران وانيران

4 منوچتري من يزدان بري شهيا وهران ملكان ملكا . . . . . .

10 ملكان ملكا . . . شهپوهري ملكان ملكا ايران وانيران

INSCRIPTION No. XIII.

In order that I may not be supposed to have neglected any of the materials within reach, for the illustration of my subject, I devote a momentary notice to the seven lines of comparatively modern Pehlvi that have been engraved upon the bas-relief (B)[1] at Firozábád. The subject of this sculpture is one of the many repetitions of the investiture of Ardeshir Babegán by Ormazd, and in itself presents little worthy of comment beyond the greater simplicity of the garments of the persons represented, and the peculiarity that Ormazd's baton is exchanged for a pointed saw-edged sword. Of the purport of the inscription, it may be as well to attempt to say nothing, as Flandin's copy is more than usually illegible, a difficulty, perhaps, inherent in the more complicated writing. The letters, where decipherable, present undoubtedly modern forms of the normal types. The epigraph has been cut in the vacant space between the Divinity and the King, and reads upwards, perpendicularly, instead of horizontally, as in the established usage. We may conclude that the inscription has been added at a period considerably later than the first execution of the sculpture, to record for posterity the interpretation put upon the tableau, while Pehlvi still continued the current language of the country.

[1] Flandin, plate 44.

The marginal engraving of a Carnelian Seal lately acquired by the British Museum (No. 12 ⁴⁄₇ 3) is inserted for the purpose of illustrating the use of the word بلكث (p. 40; Hyde, p. 358, "*Bilagh*, quorum hoc ultimatum magis peculiariter *Flammam* notare videtur"). The woodcut has been executed in Germany, but it must be confessed that much of the strange presentation of the device is due to the conventional treatment of the original gem, rather than to the shortcomings of the modern artist.

The stone, moreover, has suffered from a fracture, which runs entirely across its surface, and is especially damaging to the forehead of the profile. The legend is as follows:

[illegible] [1]

ودود زن شهپوهري زي ايرانان بلك بتي

"*Attestation of Shahpur, Fire-priest of the Iranians.*"

The only word in this epigraph which presents any difficulty is the ودود, which I suppose to be a Pehlvi modification from the Hebrew root עוד, "to return," "to say again and again," hence "to testify." But looking to the unusual size of this and of the second seal here noticed, which may be supposed to indicate the exalted position of their owners, it might be possible to interpret the original Pehlvi word by some indication of acceptance, recognition, or confirmation of a compact,

[1] The font of Pehlvi here employed has lately been commissioned from Vienna, with a view to render Mr. Austin's Printing Establishment independent of the single case of Pehlvi type in this country, heretofore made use of in this essay, in regard to the loan of which some difficulty has been created. It will be seen how very inadequately the former fulfils the duty of representing the ancient character, which is far more legible and exact in its powers of definition than the modern production which sufficed for the obscured knowledge of the Parsees of Bombay. Immediate steps will be taken for engraving discriminating letters for ג, ﺧﻪ, and ﻗﻠﻢ, and likewise for marking the difference between ا and ز, which at present are both dependent upon the simple ﺎ.

or other graduated expression of sanction on the part of an Oriental superior, and thus to refer the وحود, to وَعْدَة, "promissum" (from وَعَدَ ,וַעַד), the Indian वायदा, "promise, agreement." Though the curtailed وِد = עֵד "a witness," on the Paris gem, No. 1339, seems directly to support the former interpretation. On other occasions we meet with داتكي, from داتن, "to give" (Journ. As. Soc. Bengal, 1840, pl. i.). راستي, "truth," occurs frequently; and من راستيبي is seen on an unpublished gem of General Cunningham's, as well as the more definite term of [illegible], مودري, मुद्रा, "a seal," which appears on a signet with the device of a lion couchant and palm tree. On a second gem, with similar emblems, the opening word seems to be [illegible] = زتكي (صدق צֶדֶק), "truth, veracity." Other doubtful readings may be cited in [illegible] = كريتن, from كردن, "to do" (J.R.A.S. xiii., gem No. 12). [illegible] = من يدي (يَدٌ *manus*), (Bibl. Imp., Paris, No. 1336). [illegible] = مسع ندا ? (فدا, פדה. "redemption, ransom"), etc.[1]

Before taking leave of the question of seals and their legends, I wish to supply an omission, and to explain why I did not cite the inscription on the Himyaritic Cylinder Seal, described by Sir H. Rawlinson (at p. 234, J.R.A.S. i. N.S.), in confirmation of the parallel antiquity of the Ethiopian writing noticed at pp. 7, 8, of this Essay. My reason may be given in but few words. I am not satisfied that the Himyaritic legend was engraved simultaneously with the rest of the device; indeed the more closely the design is examined the more it becomes evident that the device and the legend are the work of different artists, and unless it may be assumed that they were engraved contemporaneously, it would scarcely be safe to rely upon the device as determining even proximately the date of the writing.

[1] See also J.R.A.S. vii. pl. 4, and Sir H. Rawlinson's valuable paper on Bilingual Cuneiform and Phœnician readings, J.R.A.S. vol. i. N.S. p. 212. And likewise, on the general subject of Sassanian Seals, Dr. A. Mordtmann's "Studien über Geschnittene Steine mit Pehlevi-Inschriften," Zeitschrift, 1864.

The singularly opportune offer of an already-prepared and hitherto-unpublished plate of coins, bearing directly upon the dynastic reconstruction of the ancient Persian empire, which it has been the object of the preceding pages to illustrate from other sources, has induced me, not unwillingly, to extend the original design of this Essay, so far as to embrace a limited series of the introductory Numismatic remains of the period, and to exemplify, by means of the coined money of the day, the transitional portraiture which maintained such typical significance in the public life of Oriental nations, as well as to complete the other more important Palæographic section of the previous investigation, by tracing through an independent class of national monuments the earlier epochs and concurrent developments of the sister alphabets under their squared and formal Numismatic aspect, as contrasted with the freedom enjoyed by the designers of the lapidary epigraphs.

Passing by the early Armenian treatment of the normal alphabet of the West, which has only an indirect bearing upon the more comprehensive range of the double set of letters of the Parthians and Persians, we find that the coins of the Arsacidæ suffice to prove, in casual but sufficiently consecutive examples, the existence of the parallel systems of Chaldæo-Pehlvi and Sassanian writing from A.D. 2 to the final extinction of the dynasty by Ardeshir Babegán in the first half of the third century. They establish further the curious coincidence of a complete disregard of any critical adherence to either one or the other approximate alphabetical systems—letters following either one form or the other seem to have been taken at hazard; and, more singular still, to have been combined in juxtaposition—sometimes one type of letter being used, sometimes the other, as if both alphabets had been in equal acceptance, whether with the ruling classes or the vulgar, for whose sake *local* writing, as opposed to the official Greek, may have been designedly employed.

There is one check and failure as yet in the evidence of the coins, in that we cannot, with any certainty, interpret their mint monograms, which clearly typified the place of issue;—these are, in truth, so susceptible of the almost endless transpositions of their crypto-characters, that the most confident Numismatists are unable to determine, with any unanimity, to what geographical section of the empire they refer; but without entering into the controversy as to whether the monogram on No. 1 symbolizes la Satrapie Apolloniatide,[1] Tambrace,[2] Assyria,[3] or other localities,[4] the coincidence of its issue by one of the members of the Bactrian branch of the Imperial Arsacidæ,[5] pushes the conjoint alphabets very far to the eastward, and leaves us to speculate vaguely upon the boundary line of Aryan Bactrian and that far earlier civilization, in Khárism, of which Sir H. Rawlinson has given us so interesting a glimpse.[6]

[1] Visconti, iii., pl. xlix., figs. 12, 15, pp. 479, 483. "ΑΠ and ΑΠΟ."

[2] Lindsay, pl. xi.

[3] D. Scott, Numismatic Chronicle, vol. xvii., p. 171.

[4] Trésor de Numismatique (M. C. Lenormant), pl. lxviii., fig. 16, p. 148. "KAT."

I must confess a preference among these readings for Tambrace. The Ταλαβρόκη in Hyrcania of Strabo (xi., c. vii., § 2). The Τάμβραξ of Polybius (x., c. 31, § 5). We find TAM and TAMB, in the form of independent letters on the obverse of the coins of the early Arsacidæ, and we meet with a more elaborated Monogram, similar to that under discussion, on the Western money of Mithridates I., which embodies every letter of the word TAMBPAX. It is possible that the traditional reverence for an early capital may have secured the perpetuation of its name among the later metropolitan cities.

[5] The Armenians, who knew more about Parthian history than other people, divided the ruling families into six branches. 1. The Parthian Arsacidæ. 2. The Armenian. Then, une troisième branche des Arsacides régnait dans le pays des Kouchans et des Thétals (ancienne Bactriane et Caboul). (M. Evariste Prud'homme, Journal Asiatique, Feb. 1866, p. 124). These latter were the kings whose successors are subsequently found reigning in the Panjáb. Wilson, Ariana Antiqua; Lassen, Ind. Alt.; Prinsep's Essays, etc.

[6] "The belief in a very early empire in Central Asia, coeval with the institution of the Assyrian monarchy, was common among the Greeks long anterior to Alexander's expedition to the East, and could only have been derived from the traditions current at the court of the Achæmenian kings. This belief, again, is connected through the names of Oxyartes and Zoroaster with the Iranian division of the Aryan race, and receives confirmation from the earliest memorials of that people . . . the opening chapters of the Vendidad indicate the progress of Iranian colonization during the earliest phases of the national existence; and it is thus of much ethnological importance to find that the empire commenced with Sogdiana, Merv, and Bactria; that in its subsequent development it included the modern provinces of Khorassan, Afghanistan, and Kharism, and finally, at its period of greatest extension, stretched from Seistan on the south, to the Jaxartes on the north, and from the Indus on the east, till it touched the extreme limit of the Median frontier to the west. It is with the Eastern Iranians, however, that we are principally concerned, as the founders of Central Asian civilization. This people, on the authority of the Vendidad, may be supposed to have achieved their first stage of development in Sughd. Their language was probably Zend, as distinguished from the Achæmenian Persian, and somewhat more removed than that dialect from the mother tongue of the Arians of the south. A more important evidence, however, of the very high state of power and civilization to which they attained is to be found in the information regarding them preserved by the cele-

The subjoined series of coins exemplify the nearly consecutive use of the fellow alphabets.

No. 1.

Silver. Size, 4½. Weight, 58 grains. B. M. *Unique.*

OBVERSE. Head of king to the left, thinly but not closely bearded, with a low Parthian tiara surmounted by two rows of studs. Monogram,  – ND.

REVERSE. The usual Parthian type of the king seated on his throne, holding out a bow. Monogram,  (*Tambrace?*).

Legend in imperfect Greek, ΒΑΣΙΛΕΥΣ ΜΕΓΑΣ ΣΑΝΑΒαρου.

Date in the field ΓΙΤ (313 of the Seleucidan era = A.D. 2.)

No. 2.

Copper. Weight, 111·5 grains. B. M. *Unique.*

OBVERSE. Head of king to the left, lightly or meagerly bearded, wearing the Parthian cap studded with jewels. Close fitting vest with jewelled collar, and a boldly ornamented border to the outer garment. *Legend.* ΒΑΣΙΛΕΥΣ μεγας.

REVERSE. Winged figure of Victory, to the right, holding out chaplet, as on the Bactrian coins of Manas, Azas, etc. *Legend.* . . . . ΣΑΝΑΒΑΡΟΥΣ.

This coin, though unpublished, has long been known, having been brought to England many years ago by Captain Hollings, of the Bengal Army. It was properly classed in the Bactrian series in the British Museum, but it was left for General Cunningham to detect its association with the quasi Parthian coin (No. 1) of the same monarch.

brated Abu Rihan, himself a native of the country, and the only Arab writer who investigated the antiquities of the East in a true spirit of historical criticism. This writer supplies us with an extensive specimen of the old dialects of Sugdh and Kharism. He gives us in those dialects the names of the twelve months, the names of the thirty days of the month, and the five Epagomenæ, together with the names of the signs of the Zodiac and of the seven planets, and lastly of the mansions of the moon. A portion of this nomenclature is original, and offers a most curious subject for investigation; but the majority of the names can be compared, as was to be expected, with the Zend correspondents, and, indeed, are much nearer to the primitive forms than are the better known Parsee equivalents. According to Abu Rihan, again, the solar calendar of Kharism was the most perfect scheme for measuring time with which he was acquainted; and it was maintained by the astronomers of that country that both the solar and lunar Zodiacs had originated with them, the divisions of the signs in their system being far more regular than those adopted by the Greeks or Arabs . . . . . . Abu Rihan asserts that the Kharismians dated originally from an epoch anterior by 980 years to the era of Seleucidæ, a date which agrees pretty accurately with the period assigned by our best scholars to the invention of the Jyotisha or Indian calendar."—*Quarterly Review*, October, 1866, p. 488, etc.

No. 3.

The next appearance of the local alphabets is on a coin of Arsaces XVI. (A.S. 316=A.D. 4), which has been published in the Révue de la Numismatique Belge (4th series, vol. iv. p. 369), and described by M. de Baron B. de Koehne, who, by a most singular hallucination, has converted the initial letters of the name of Arsaces (אר) on the *reverse* into the Greek characters ΠΣ, or, in their capacity of numerals, into the figures for 280; and as he had already been obliged to recognise the proper Seleucidan date of ΤΙϚ=315 on the obverse, he proceeded to propound an elaborate theory, which was to set at rest that still undetermined problem, the true initial epoch of the Arsacidæ, by the aid of the numbers expressed in the conjoint dates. The *obverse* of this coin presents the head of Arsaces Phraatacos, with the numeral letters ΤΙϚ on the flowing fillet at the back. The *reverse* displays the head Mousa,[1] the Queen Mother, with the Greek letters ΘΕΑΣ on the margin, outside the fillets, and between the fillets and the Queen's neck, looking at the coin from the same point of view as is necessary to make the Greek legible, there are seen in a parallel line, though reading from the opposite direction, the two Chaldæo-Pehlvi letters אר *ar*. The first of which partakes somewhat of the Sassanian form of the character *a*, while the ר is more like a Chaldæo-Pehlvi ג *g* or כ *k*, an outline the Parthian ר *r* was frequently made to follow, as may be seen in examples of the bronze coins described below, under No. 9,[2] as well as in the curious developments of the *r* on the money of Artavasdes, No. 13. If there were any doubt about the propriety of reading these letters as the initials of a name, it would be set at rest by the location of the monogrammatic symbol for the name of *Mousa*, which is inserted in exactly the same position, in proximity to the Queen's head, on the coins of Phraates IV. A coin of this Prince, figured by M. de Longpérier, which marks the first introduction of the bust of a female on the Parthian currency, seems to have been influenced in its details by some Oriental reserve in regard to so decided an innovation; and though the word ΘΕΑΣ is inserted in

[1] The Italian slave "*Thermusa*" of Josephus, xviii., c. ii., § 4. The name is indubitably S. मूषक, H. موسا, P. موش, *mûs*, *mus*, "a mouse." A designation still largely affected by Hindu Anonyma.

[2] See also Numismatic Chronicle, xii., plate, fig. 1, p. 84; xvii., 167; Longpérier, pl. xviii.; Dr. Levy, Zeitschrift, 1867, pl. ii., fig. 13.

the margin, the name of the favourite is subdued into the elegant monogram , which, however, clearly embraces all the letters of the word ΜΟΥΣΑΣ.[1] In coins of a later period, all disguise is laid aside; and although the identical monogram is retained in its original position, Mousa's name and titles are given in full, as ΘΕΑϹ ΟΥΡΑΝΙΑϹ ΜΟΥϹΗϹ ΒΑϹΙΛ [ισσης]. Epithets she certainly did not deserve, if we are to credit Josephus.

It may seem over-venturesome for one who has not seen the coin itself to attempt to correct the reading of so high an authority as M. de Koehne, who has had the piece under close and deliberate examination; but the truth is, the suggestion of the discovery of any new system of dating in the East has such charms for those who are enquiring into the primitive condition of Central Asia, that I tested every possible solar and lunar variety of methods of calculation to see if this new theory would hold water; but as these comparisons all ended in simple chaos, there can be little objection to submitting the leading evidence to a more practical and mechanical proof.

No. 4.

Vologeses I. (A.D. 52 to 60). "Buste barbu et diadémé de Vologèse, à dr., une verrue au front, la barbe moins longue que celle de Gotarzes, mais coupée de la même manière; derr. VOL en caract. araméens.

Rev. 1. ΒΑϹΙΛΕΩϹ ΒΑϹΙΛΕΩΝ. 2. ΑΡϹΑΚΟΥ. 3. ΕΥΕΡΓΕΤΟΥ. ΔΙΚΑΙΟΥ. 4. ΕΠΙΦΑΝΟΥΣ ΦΙΛΕΛΛΗΝ. Le roi assis, à dr., tenant l'arc; dans le champ, ΤΑ.

Being unable to refer to any original coins of this particular type, I had sedulously transcribed the above description from M. Rollin's "Sale Catalogue," under the impression that M. de Longpérier, having withdrawn from circulation, as far as he was able, all copies of his Mémoires . . des "Rois Parthes Arsacides" (Rollin, Paris, 1857), was desirous that the work should be altogether ignored by those who might have access to impressions still unredeemed and at large; but the Publisher's note at p. 541 of the Catalogue[2] seems to relieve me of any such needless reserve; and

[1] ΜΟΥΣΑΣ and ΜΟΥΣΗΣ were used indifferently on the coins.—Lindsay, pl. iii., figs. 62, 63, and p. 171.

[2] "C'est encore à M. de Longpérier que la science est redevable de la découverte de ces légendes araméennes, dès l'année 1841, dans la Revue de Numismatique française, pages 250 et 261. Le savant académicien faisait pressentir sa précieuse

though I should hesitate to criticise, in any adverse sense, a confessedly incomplete production, it would be unfair to conceal my knowledge of its contents, or to fail to express my great regret that such an accumulation of choice materials should even temporarily be withheld from the general public. At the same time, recognising the excellence of the plates, I hold myself altogether free to draw my own independent deductions from the facsimiles, as if I were inspecting the coins themselves, though I pass by the text, even where I have examined it, as if it were still unwritten.

No. 5.

M. de Longpérier's plate, No. xiv., fig. 10, is a copy of another coin, with the letters ול on the obverse, which is not noticed in M. Rollin's Catalogue, but which the author seems to attribute to Vologeses III., as he makes the king of that name, whom Mr. Lindsay supposed to be Vologeses III., into Vologeses IV., and so on in succession, advancing the numbers throughout the series, a process which is necessitated by the discovery of a new Vologeses II. The coin in question is similar in its typical details to that engraved by Mr. Lindsay under No. 86, pl. iv., and is marked by the peculiar tiara, with curled ornaments over the ridge, which is held to be special to this king in his silver currency.

No. 6.

Mithridates. The usual size. Weight, 53 grains. B. M.

Obverse. Head of king, with formally pointed beard, flowing hair behind, but flat on the top of the head above the diadem.

Reverse. King seated on his throne extending a bow.

Legend. At the top מתרדת מלכא. *Mitradat Malka.* Imperfect Greek on four sides, 1. ΒΑΙΛΑΕΑ. 2. ΙΙΑΝΟΥ. 3. ΕΤΙΙΓΙΤ ΔΕΙΑΟΥ. 4. ΠΦΑΝΙΟΥΣ ΤΦΑΙΛΑΗΕ.

One coin, B.M. A second coin of *Gen. Cunningham's* is engraved in Longpérier's plates, and is noticed in Rollin's Catalogue under No. 6053. A third coin is also engraved in M. de Longpérier's work. The date of this reign is supposed to be after 418 up to 424.

No. 7. Vologeses IV. Silver.

Obverse. Head similar to that engraved under No. 87, pl. iv.

découverte dans son grand ouvrage qui, à si juste titre, a obtenu le grand prix de numismatique. Il donne six rois différents, et tous ont le titre de Malca, faisant suite à leur nom propre."

Lindsay. On the field the letters ול, or properly speaking ول, for the *vav* follows the Chaldæo-Pehlvi model, while the *lam*, in this instance, is clearly and essentially after the Sassanian form of that consonant.

Reverse. The conventional type of the enthroned Parthian monarch, extending a bow, associated with the usual degraded Greek legends and the monogram for *Tambrace*.

B. M. Two coins. Dates on the larger coins extend from 389 to 439 A.S.

No. 8.

Vologeses IV. Silver.

Obverse. King's head, as in the engraving.[1]

Reverse. The usual type with the debased Greek legends, but the opening ΒΑΣΙΛΕΩΣ in the top line is replaced by the Chaldæo-Pehlvi ולגשי מלכא *Valgashi Malka*, "Vologeses king."

Monograms, TA.

The Greek has been omitted in the cut.

Nine coins in the B. M. Dates range from 460 to 488 A.S.

No. 9.

Vologeses IV. Bronze. Weight, 104 grains.

Obverse. King's head with the usual tiara. Monogram, a Greek *B*.

Reverse. Device, ♀, forming a square, around which is the legend ולגשי ארשך מלכין מלכא (ولگشي ارشك ملكين ملكا). Vologeses, Arsaces, king of kings.

I believe I may claim to have been the first to publish decipherments of these legends.[2] They are chiefly remarkable in reference to the present enquiry, as demonstrating a determination on the part of the ruling authorities of the day to emancipate themselves

[1] I am indebted to that enthusiastic Numismatist, Richard Sainthill, Esq., of Cork, for the loan of the above, and of the second similar wood engraving, both of which originally appeared in his "Olla Podrida," London, 1853, vol. ii., p. xxii.

[2] Numismatic Chronicle, xii. (1849), p. 84; xvii. 161, etc.

from the scarcely intelligible Greek, which had sunk into a state of complete degradation in its exotic life on Eastern soil, and to reclaim due priority for the local language and alphabet. The distinctive symbol on the reverse, which has been the subject of much discussion,[1] I conceive to have been the more conventional representation of the Sun, based upon ancient models, the worship of which was largely affected by the Arsacidæ.[2] The earliest symbol of the Sun, under the first Chaldæan monarchy, consisted of a simple circle, which in advancing ornamentation was divided into four quarters ⊕, and ultimately improved into something in the form of a flower.[3] The primary idea is preserved in עגל בעל "Dominus rotundus,"[4] and its effective use under some such form of the figure of the Sun is testified to in the "Imago Solis," which we are told formed so prominent an object in the ceremonial processions of Darius Codomannus.[5] The same simple round orb is used to represent the Sun on the sculptured monuments of Persepolis, where, in the bas-reliefs which ornament each Achæmenian king's tomb, "Mithra" is exhibited in a prominent position in the heavens to the front of the Fire Altar.[6] The old symbol seems to have undergone many modifications, according to local treatment, which it is scarcely necessary to trace in this place,[7] but I may advert to its appearance as the leading symbol on a standard of the Sassanian period, where placed upon a lance-pole and supplemented by a cross bar with flowing horse tails, it is borne in the front of the battle.[8]

[1] Pellerin, 3rd Supplement, p. 82; Mionnet, v. p. 686; M. de Luynes', Coins of "Soli," Fasti, p. 61; Ariana Antiqua, pl. xv. fig. 9.

[2] Moses Khor., French edition, i. 163 and 337.

[3] Ancient Monarchies, G. Rawlinson, i. 159; Layard's Nineveh (1853), p. 211.

[4] Selden, 223; Hyde, 114.

[5] Patrio more Persarum traditum est, orto sole demum procedere. Die jam illustri signum e tabernaculo regis bucina dabatur. Super tabernaculum, unde ab omnibus conspici posset, imago solis crystallo inclusa fulgebat.—Quintus Curtius, iii. c. 3, § 7.

[6] See Ker Porter, pl. xvii. p. 519; Flandin, plates 164 *bis*, 166, 172, 174, 175, 176, 178.

[7] Texier, Asie Mineure (Petrium), plates 78-6-7-8-9; Layard's Nineveh and its Remains, ii. 212, 456; Donaldson, Architectura Numismatica, pp. 23, 72; El Gabal (Jupiter Sol) at Emesa, A.D. 222, pp. 76, 80, 88, 98, 105, 106, 127, 150, 230; Levy, Phön. Studien, p. 37; L. Muller, pl. ix. (Tricca); Marsden, Numismata Orientalia, pl. xvii. figs. 1-7; De Saulcy, Journal Asiatique, 3me serie (1839), 1re Lettre; Longpérier, pl. xvii.; Das Labarum und Der Sonnen-Cultus. Edward Rapp. Bonn, 1865. Lajard, Culte de Mithra, pl. xxxv. *et seq.*

[8] Ker Porter, pl. xx; Flandin, 184.

No. 10. Vologeses V.

Obverse. Front face, with bushy side curls. Lindsay. Fig. 93, pl, iv.

Reverse. Similar legends and monogram for Tambraco; but the letters both in the Greek and the Chaldæo-Pehlvi, are even more imperfectly formed and straggling than on previous coinages.

Dates range from 502 to 520.

No. 11. Vologeses VI.

Obverse. Profile of king (Lindsay, Nos. 94, 96, pl. iv.) with the letters ול in the field. The tiara of this king, as well as those of Artavasdes, are marked by an ornamental spiked or feathered bar running up the side of the helmet.

Reverse. Type and legends as in the silver coins of Vologeses IV. Six coins B. M.

Dates range from 521 to 538 A.S.

No. 12. Artabanus V.

Obverse. Head of king, with a plain side bar on the tiara, which is less elevated, or, rather, more encroached upon by the succession of fillets than usual.

Reverse. The usual type and debased Greek legends with the Chaldæo-Pehlvi. הרתבי מלכא in the top line.

Seven coins in the B.M. Dates range from 521 to 538 A.S.

No. 13. Artavasdes.

Obverse. Head of the king distinguished by a parted beard and feathered bar on the tiara (Lindsay, No. 95, pl. iv.) behind the head in the field the Chaldæo-Pehlvi letters אר.

Reverse. The usual type and debased legends, with traces of ארתבזו מלכא (Mr. Lindsay's coin is more legible than the Engraver has made it appear).

Two coins, B.M. Date 559 A.S.

It is curious to observe the contrast in the spelling in the initial portion of these names of Artabanus and Artavasdes. The *Hartabi* of the former seems to have been imitated from the oral sound of the Greek Ἀρτάβαζος, while the Artabazú is clearly the proper Persian form of the name ارت بازو[1] "strong arm," as we have the proximate synonyms תריבזו and פרנבזו on the coins of the Achæmenian Satraps, Tiribazes and Pharnabazes.

SUB-PARTHIAN COINS.

No. 14. Silver. Weight, 25 grs. D. M. Two coins. Pl. fig. 3.

Obverse. Head of king to the left, similar in its details to certain examples of the portrait of Phraates IV.[2] Crescent (and star?) in the field.

Legend, in mixed Chaldæo and Sassanian Pehlvi, ... ארתהשתר מ ارتهشتر مــــ.

Reverse. Crowned head to the left.

Legend, in Sassanian Pehlvi, ملكين . . . ملكا? The suggested ملكين may be possibly read as منشتري for منوشتري?

No. 15, Silver. Plate, fig. 4.

Obverse. Head to the left, with Parthian tiara.

Legend. اتوردت ملكا = ... ?

Reverse. Head to the left, with head-dress arranged after the manner but slightly differing from Arsacidan models.

Legend, imperfect. — — بري — ملكا —

Other obverse devices of similar character, conjoined with a reverse Arab head, like the above, but altogether wanting in the circular legend, display the title of ارتهشتر ملكا N. C. xii. fig. 3; while the legends on the reverse of a similar coin (Num. Chron. xii. fig. 4) seem to run כואת מלכא ברי כמיות מלכא, "Kobád, king, son of Kamiút, king"

· No. 16. Silver. Weight. Plate, fig. 5.

Obverse. Head with Parthian tiara, ornamented with a crescent and a star, to the left.

Legend. Obscure.

Reverse. Head with the hair arranged after an exceptional Arsacidan fashion.

Legend. شتري سان — — — —?

[1] M. de Luynes, Pl. i., figs. 1-3, 4, etc., ارت magnus. ... Zend *areta*, ἀρτα ('Ἀρταῖοι, Herodotus, vii. 61) and بازو. ... brachium.

[2] Lindsay, iii. 52; Longpérier, ix. 9.

I had intended to have passed over the Sub-Parthian series of coins with but scant comment, as the peculiarly degraded forms of the letters employed gave but little promise of legitimate Palæographic illustration, but the unexpected discovery of the correct attribution of an extensive class of these mintages throws new light, both historical and geographical, on the general inquiry.

A short time ago, General Cunningham, knowing that I was interested in these medals, was kind enough to bring me three pieces of the type D, on one of which was clearly defined the ordinarily-bungled and unintelligible Greek monogram  a combination that proved readily susceptible of being expanded into the full name of ΑΤΡΟΠΑΤΗΝΗ. The next step in the solution of the problem was to enquire whether any and what kings claimed, during the Parthian sway, the country of Azerbaiján. A branch of a family tree opportunely presented itself in the record of two reigns in Atropatenian Media, which had been casually adverted to by classical writers, in connexion with the wars of Lucullus and Antony in the East;[1] and, singular to say, the two designations thus preserved, approximately accorded with two of the three successions perpetuated on the coins, viz., those of the father and son, Darius and Artaxerxes. The third but earliest of the race is called יתורדת *Atúrdat*, "Gift of Fire," (Ἀτραδάτης),[2] an association which, however strange to modern ears, is strictly emblematic of the early Zoroastrian creed, and clearly in unison with the parallel nomenclature of Mithridates and Tiridates. The name itself is probably identical with the Armenian *Ardoates* or *Artovart*,[3] which seem to have been corrupt transcriptions of the original Oriental term, which is more accurately reproduced in the Pehlvi 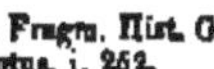 (اتور دات) and 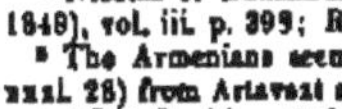 (اتور يزدان دات) of the Sassanian Seals.[4]

We have no collateral evidence of the existence of this particular *Atúrdat*, but he may be conjectured to have been some relative of the great *Tigranes* of Armenia, and by him entrusted with the

[1] Sir H. Rawlinson, Journ. Roy. Geog. Soc. x. p. 65; Masson, J.R.A.S. xii. pp. 97, 123.

[2] Nicolas of Damascus, quoting Ctesias. Fragm. Hist. Græc. (C. Müller, Paris, 1849), vol. iii. p. 399; Rawlinson's Herodotus, i. 252.

[3] The Armenians seem fully to discriminate Artovart (Ἀρδοάτης, Diod. Sic. xxxi. 28) from Artavazt and Arduschas. St. Martin. i. 409.

[4] J.R.A.S. xiii. p. 245, gems Nos. 63, 68.

charge of Atropatene on its conquest.[1] Though Strabo[2] is most distinct in his assertion that the successors of Atropates[3] continued in independent possession of the country up to, and after the commencement of the Christian era, and it might be inferred from his expressions that they strengthened their position from time to time by matrimonial alliances with the Kings of Armenia, Syria, and Parthia; it is possible that, in all cases, the local king may have been permitted to retain the government, subject to the acknowledgment of fealty to the Suzerain of the day, whether Armenian or Parthian. However, be this as it may, we find Atúrdat's son Darius, or *Dárīl* (Dárir), as he calls himself on the coins, fully established as king of Northern Media in B.C. 69.[4] The appearance of a close copy of the head of Mithridates I. of Parthia (B.C. 173-136) on the obverse of the coins, may be taken to imply that Darius recognized him as the common ancestor of the dynasty, and the real founder of the Arsacidan empire.[5] Tigranes the great is supposed by some authors to have been a descendant of Artaxias, but we know that Volarsaces I. (B.C. 149-127), the great-grandfather of Tigranes, was placed upon the throne of Armenia by his own brother Mithridates I. of Parthia,[6] which would seem to establish a totally different relationship, unless we may infer a descent from Artaxias by the mother's side. But under any circumstances the imitation of the style of the great conqueror on the coins of his successors, in the conjoint Armenian branches

[1] Strabo, xi. c. xiv. § 15; St. Martin, I. 291, 410. [2] Book xi. c. xiii. § 1.

[3] The name seems to be merely *Atár-Pati* (पति), so also the word Atropatene may have something in common with [illegible] ([illegible] to surround, to encompass), in which case the synonym 'Αγβάτανα would respond to अग्नि ([illegible]) Ignis, آگ "fire," *Ag-patana*, the *Hagmatana* of the Assyrian Cuneiform: an etymology which would sufficiently account for the frequent application of the name to the sacred places of the Persians. (*Cf.* 'Αγβάτανα. Strabo, xv. c. iii. § 6.)

[4] Ὁ δὲ Πομπήιος καὶ τὸν Ταῦρον ὑπερελθὼν, ἐπολέμησεν Ἀντιόχῳ τῷ Κομμαγηνῷ, ἕως ἐς φιλίαν ὁ Ἀντίοχος αὐτῷ συνῆλθεν. ἐπολέμησε δὲ καὶ Δαρείῳ τῷ Μήδῳ, μέχρις ἔφυγεν, εἴτε Ἀντιόχῳ συμμαχῶν, εἴτε Τιγράνῃ πρότερον.—Appian. Mith. cvi.
ΔΑΡΕΙΟΣ ΜΗΔΟΣ is also mentioned in the triumph of Pompey as one of the kings conquered during the war.—App. Mith. cxvi.

[5] M. F. Lenormant had already recognised the likeness of the head on the obverse of these coins to that of Mithridates I., as he is conventionally portrayed on a special class of his own proper currency, a similitude which was obvious and self-evident, though not obviously material (Journal Asiatique, 1865, page 205). But the appearance of the effigy of the effective founder of the Parthian Empire no more implies contemporaneity, than does a similar imitation by Ardeshír Babegán, so many centuries later, carry any epochal value.

[6] St. Martin specially mentions that the kingdom, thus established, embraced Atropatene; i. p. 289.

of the family, was quite consistent with the known reverence entertained by the Parthians for their ancestors, and the special feeling that none but the members of the family of the Arsacidæ were fit to reign. The portrait, it is true, is probably intended to represent Darius himself, though much of the likeness of the original profile is preserved, but the symbol of the half-moon upon Darius' tiara indicates alike his Armenian connexion, and marks the contrast with the star which forms the central ornament of the helmet of Mithridates I.[1] The proper Armenian coins of a king calling himself, in similar orthography, Atúrdat, also exhibit on the obverse of the earlier examples, a bust, very similar to that of Mithridates I, as it is figured on the larger pieces of the Western mints,[2] with the head uncovered and the hair merely retained by the fillet. The same local sovereign's name also appears on another class of the Armenian currency, which is distinguished by a Romanized form of the ancient Phrygo-Armenian or Mosynœcian helmet,[3] surmounted by a crescent, which latter takes the place of the Roman eagle, that constitutes the crest in previous mintages. Another set of coins which connect themselves in their reverse types with Atúrdat's money, bear the name of Tiridates (תירדת) in Chaldæo-Pehlvi, having an associate obverse device of the same uncovered head of the Mithridates style. The reverses of the Armenian coins present a different type of Fire Altar to that employed by the Atropatenians. Originally the reverse design consisted of a built-up pedestal of the height of a man, having three small altars on the top, with the King or Mobed on one side and the curious Cuneiform symbol for an Altar,[4] in the form of a standard, on the other. Gradually the design of the Fire-temple is modified by the introduction of the figure of Ormazd issuing from the flames, and subsequently, as the worship of Venus, or Luna, grew upon the purer Zoroastrianism, the side altar is surmounted by a Cock,[5] and the device assumes a near identity with

[1] Lindsay, Pl. i., figs. 19, 20; Trésor de Numismatique, Pl. lxvii., fig. 13; Longpérier, Pl. iii.

[2] Trésor de Numismatique, lxvii., fig. 10; Longpérier, Pl. iii.

[3] Herodotus, vii., 61, 62, 72; Xenophon, Anab. V. c. iv., § 13; Num. Chron.

[4] G. Rawlinson's Ancient Monarchies I., p. 337; Num. Chron., N.S., vii., (1867), p. 236.

[5] Selden, De Diis Syris, 309; Haugh, 213. The services rendered by the Cock (Parô-dars), the bird of Serosh., 18th Fargard. Z.A. M. Vámbéry in his "Sketches of "Central Asia" (London, 1868), mentions that to this day in Bokhára, a cock is offered on the Nauruz "by *all* Fire Worshippers."

the Ancient Babylonian illustration of the worship of the Moon,[1] which has been preserved on one of the Seal Cylinders discovered by Mr. Layard.

The son of Darir, who is entitled Ardeshir on the coins, may fairly be identified with the king designated by Dion Cassius as the Ἀρταουάσδης[2] of Northern Media, at the period of Antony's invasion of that province in 36 B.C. The general character of the coins, in fabric, types and forms of letters, coincides completely with the issues of Darir, the one exception being that Ardeshir introduces the striking novelty among Oriental peoples of a veritable well-formed coronet crown, which seems to have been imitated from the "Corona Muralis" of the Romans, with this improvement, however, that whereas the Western model was formed of a mere succession of towers with triple pinnæ, which had an air of much sameness, the Eastern coronet was designed after their own system of battlements of three gradational steps, which produced a much more open and bold effect. How the King of the Medes of those days came to affect such a head-dress it would be rash to say, but there may have been a vague design and a covert taunt in the Oriental mind which suggested the assumption of the Mural crown that the defender of the enceinte of Phraata[3] so well deserved. Though it is possible that the subsequently friendly relations established between Antony and the same King of the Medes[4] may have had something to do with the foreign adaptation.

[1] Layard, Nineveh, pp. 538, 539; King's Gems, pp. 129, 137. Strabo (xi. c. xiv. § 16) specially mentions that the Armenians had associated with their system of Fire-worship great reverence for Anaïtis, and had built numerous temples to her honour.

[2] Καὶ ἦλθε μέχρι τοῦ Εὐφράτου, νομίζων ἔρημον αὐτὸν φρουρᾶς εἶναι· ἐπεὶ μέντοι πάντα τὰ ταύτῃ διὰ φυλακῆς ἀκριβοῦς ὄντα εὗρεν, ἐκεῖθεν μὲν ἀνετράπετο, ἐπὶ δὲ τὸν τῶν Μήδων βασιλέα Ἀρταουάσδην τῷ τῆς Ἀρμενίας τῆς μείζονος βασιλεῖ, ὁμωνύμῳ τέ οἱ καὶ ἐχθρῷ ὄντι, πεισθεὶς στρατεῦσαι, πρὸς τὴν Ἀρμενίαν εὐθὺς ὥσπερ εἶχεν ἐχώρησε.—Dion Cass. xlix. 25. [Editor's note] Alii Ἀρτάβαζον habent. See also xlix. 33, 40, 44, and li. 16.

[3] Sir H. Rawlinson in his exhaustive Memoir on the site of the Atropatenian Ecbatana (Journ. Roy. Geog. Soc., x., p. 65), has traced, with much care the new names assigned at various epochs to the "Seven-walled City" of Dejoces, Ecbatana, Phraata, Praaspa, Vera, Gaza, Gazaca, Canzaca (Kandeg), Azergushasp, Azerbádegan, Atún-Pádegán, Azerekhsh (Derekhsh), Shíz (Arrian), Takht-i-Soleïmán. See also Strabo, xi. c. xiii. § 3; Ker Porter, ii. 97.

[4] Plutarch in Antony.

DARIUS, KING OF MEDIA ATROPATENE.

CLASS A.—Silver.

OBVERSE. Head similar to that of Mithridates I.[1] with the the Parthian tiara, with the side ornament of a half moon.

No legend.

REVERSE. *Device:* A Mobed ministering before a small Fire Altar.

Legend. דאריל מלכא בריי יתורדת מלכא.

Dáril, king, son of Itúrdat, king.

CLASS A. *a.*—There is a parallel series of coins of this prince with a similar reverse device (but with far more crude legends), which are remarkable as having a coarse Parthian head on the obverse, something in the style of the portraits of Phraates II. These pieces probably belonged to a different division of the kingdom of Northern Media. There are, at times, traces of a name on the obverse, but the specimens available do not suffice to determine its purport.

CLASS A. *b.*—Daril's name occurs also on a coin, in the East India Collection, having on the

OBVERSE. A Parthian head.

REVERSE. A small standing figure, with a star and crescent to the front (similar to the reverse figured under No. 4, Plate xv. Ariana Antiqua).

Legend. דאריל מלכא.

ARDESHIR, SON OF DARIUS, KING OF MEDIA ATROPATENE.

CLASS B. Silver. Weight, 63 grains. B.M.[2]

OBVERSE. Head of the King[3] wearing a crown, similar to that on No. 3 of the accompanying Plate, but more highly finished.

(No legend.) Traces of a similar monogram to that above noticed.

[1] For engravings of similar coins see Ariana Antiqua, pl. xv. fig. 2; Numismatic Chronicle, vol. xii. pl., p. 68, figs. 5, 6, 7; Lindsay, pl. x. figs. 27, 28; Zeitschrift, vol. xxi. pl. ii. figs. 2, 3, 4, 5.

[2] There are great varieties of sizes and weights of this issue, indicating a complete and comprehensive system of currency,—the smaller pieces go down as low as 9 grains.

[3] For engravings of similar coins see Ariana Antiqua, pl. xv. fig. 3; Num. Chron. xii. pl. fig. 8; Zeitschrift, vol. xxi. pl. ii. figs. 9, 10.

Reverse. *Device:* A Mobed ministering before a Fire Altar.

Legend.  (*Facsimile*).

ארתחשתר מלכא ברײ דארלי מלכא Hebrew.

Class B. a.—As in the case of his father, Ardeshir likewise issued a series of coins of inferior execution, with a coarse type of an uncovered Parthian head.

SASSANIAN COINS.

No. 17. No. 1 plate. Silver.

Obverse. Front face of Ardeshir.

Legend. 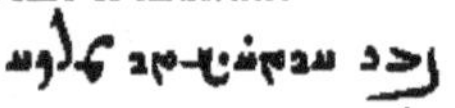 Pehlvi.

بگي ارتهشـــتر ملكا In modern Persian.

Reverse. Profile head of Papak, with the Parthian helmet.

Legend. 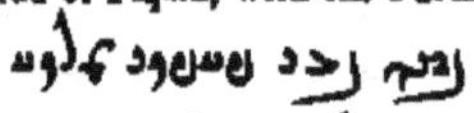 Pehlvi.

بري بگي پابكي ملكا Persian.

Other specimens of this class of coin are to be found in the B. M., silver, weight, 58 grs.; East India collection; and a third, to which I cannot now refer, once in the possession of Mr. Luscombe. The earliest decipherment of these coins is due to M. M. Dorn and Bartholomaei, who published notices of their readings in the Mémoires de la Société d' Archéologie of St. Petersburg in 1847. My interpretation differs but slightly from that originally given.

No. 18. No. 6 plate. Silver. Weight of the best specimen, 65·5 grs.

Obverse. Head of king to the right.

Legend.

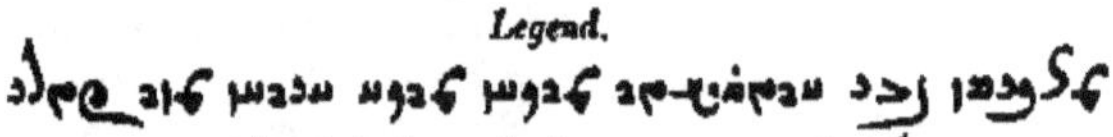

مزديسن بگي ارتهشـــتر مركان مركا ايران منوچتري

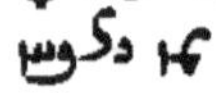

من يزدان

Reverse. A Fire Altar.

Legend. 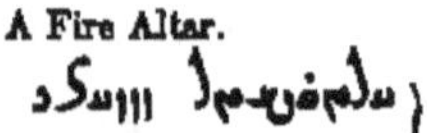 ارتهشـــتر نوازي } Ardeshir's Fire-temple.

No. 19. No. 7 plate. Weights average from 63 to 64 grs. Coin nearly identical with No. 6 plate.

No. 20. No. 8 plate. Weight, 32·0 grs. Ditto.

No. 21. No. 9 plate. Weight, 9·5 grs. Ditto.

No. 22. No. 10 plate. Silver. Weight, 60·0 grs. B. M.

Obverse. King's head to the right, wearing a highly ornamented Parthian tiara, exactly similar to the pattern in use under Mithridates I.[1]

Legend. 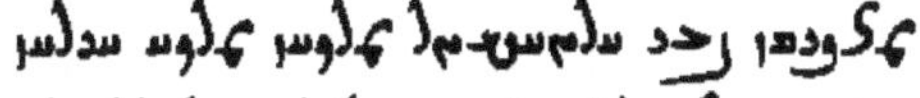

مزدیسن بگي ارتهشتر مرکان مرکا ایران

Reverse. The usual Fire Altar, with 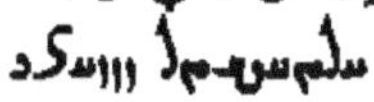

ارتهشتر نووازي

There is a choice gold piece of this type in the British Museum (weight, 131 grains), an engraving of which is to be found in the Numismatic Chronicle, vol. xv., and which has been copied in plate x. of the Zeitschrift for 1854.

No. 23. Plate, No. 11.

Coin of the same king of a similar character, in *billon*. The legends are coarser and necessarily less complete. A second more legible specimen in the B.M. supplies the following reading:

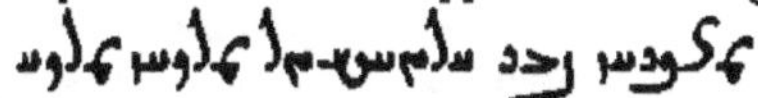

The variations in the types of Ardeshir's coins will be seen to illustrate, in curious completeness, the progressive extension of his dominions. As step by step he exterminated the surviving branches of the Arsacidan dynasty, he marked each conquest by the reproduction of the typical emblems of the fallen monarchy on the new issues of public money. In effect, he seems to have aimed at a numismatic exhibition of a series of royal portraits, not the likenesses of his own ancestors, but the conventional effigies of the enemies of his race, from whom he eventually regained the old dominion of Darius, commencing with his first great success over Vologeses, the reigning king of the southern division of the Parthian dominions, and ending with the triumphant recovery of the sacred Fire-Altar of Atropatene and the rest of their domains

[1] Visconti, pl. 48, fig. 6; Trésor de Numismatique, pl. lxvii. fig. 13; Longpérier, pl. lii. fig. 9.

from the Armenian Arsacidæ, an event which is further commemorated in the extant bas-relief at Salmas,[1] where Ardeshir and his son Sapor are depicted as Lords of the bushy-haired Armenians,[2] one of whom stands at the bridle rein of each victor's horse.

Ardeshir's earliest coinage (No. 17, Plate No. 1) clearly imitates, in the treatment of the head-dress, the recognised style of the front face of Vologeses V. (No. 10). This assimilation may either refer to his assumption of the Sovereignty of Johar, the Arsacidan local ruler of Persepolis,[3] during the life-time of Vologeses V., or may, perhaps, be designed to indicate the later defeat of Vologeses VI. in Kermán. The next gradation in the progress of the State currency is indicated by Ardeshir's modified reproduction of the archaic plaited hair and beard, Nos. 18, 19, 20, 21 (Nos. 6, 7, 8, 9 plate), which was probably intended to denote the reassertion of the ancient Persian empire, combined with the reverse device of the new Zoroastrianism matured amid the Fire-temples of the South. The original Parthian tiara of Mithridates I. (B.C. 173, 136), which appears on the coins Nos. 22, 23 (Nos. 10, 11 plate), is associated with an absolute likeness of that great conqueror, who, in effect, raised the Parthian monarchy to the higher degree of the Arsacidan empire. There can be no question, in this instance, as to the modern profile, which is absolutely identical with some of the more finished portraits of Mithridates I. on his own proper coins of four centuries' prior date. It is evident that the head of the Sassanian period was an intentional copy of the old model, and it is in no wise to be confounded with any attempt at a subdued likeness of Ardeshir himself, whose type of countenance will be seen to differ entirely, both in the numismatic and sculptured examples, from the physiognomy of the Parthian Emperor; while Ardeshir's name and titles which surround the central device declare his accession to the supreme authority, and the fall of the last scion of the house of Arsaces, the bust of whose

[1] Ker Porter, pl. 82, vol. ii., 597; Flandin, pls. 204, 205; St. Martin, i. 179; Morier, p. 299.

[2] . . . . mistis hic Colchus Hiberis,
Hic Mitra velatus Arabs, hic crine decoro
Armenius; hic picta Saces, fucataque Medus.
—Claudian, sal. 165.

[3] Tabari MS. Ibn Athir (Tornberg, 1867), vol. i. p. 272; Shâh Nâmah (Macan) iii. p. 1366; Hamza Ispahani, p. 31; De Sacy, pp. 32, 167, 374; Journal Asiatique, vii. (1839), p. 270.

SASSANIAN COINS.

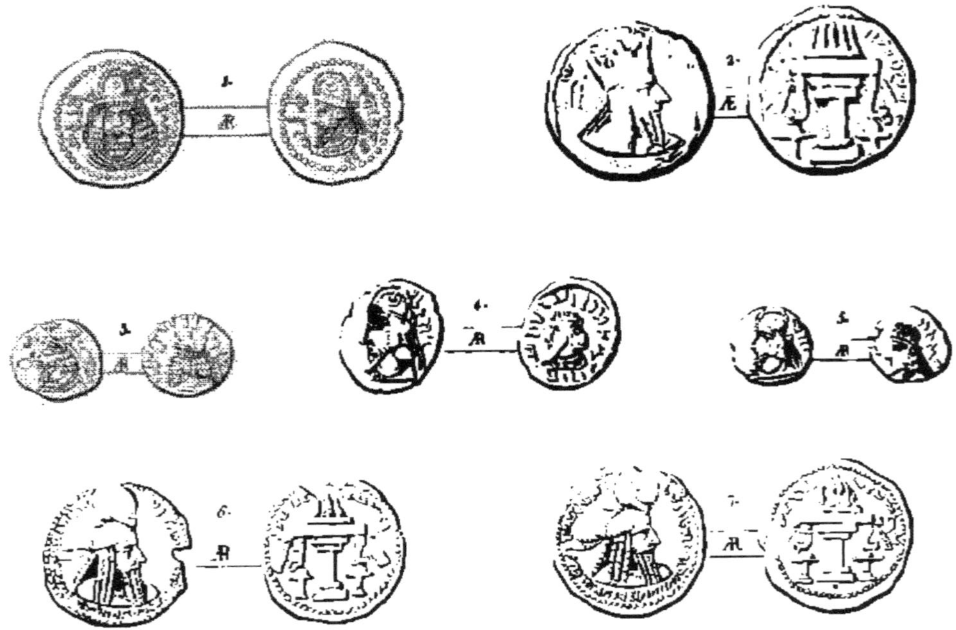

8.

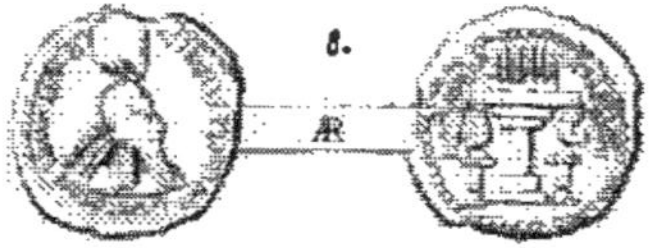

9.

10.

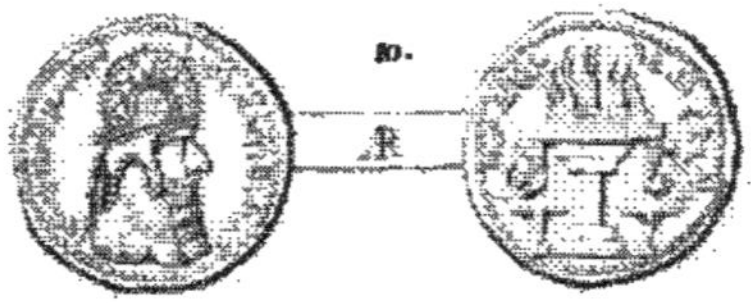

11.

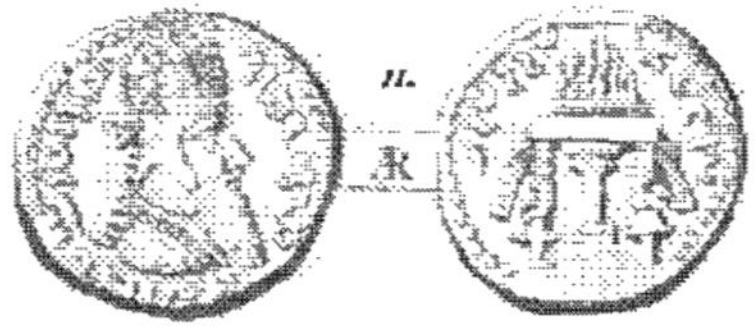

12.

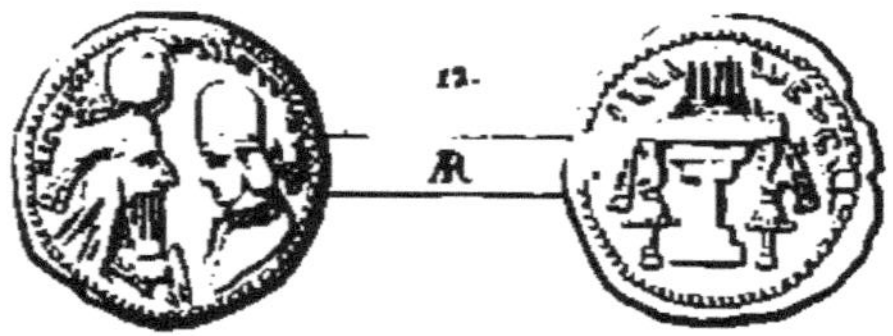

And. Russo dis. ed inc.

most prominent ancestor appears upon the field, and on the reverse the new symbol of the Sassanian Fire-Altar supersedes the Parthian bowman. These changes of course point to Ardeshir's final conquest over Ardeván and the consolidation of the revived Persian monarchy. The latest development of emblematic varieties is to be found in the mural crown adopted by Ardeshir and copied by Sapor (coin No. 25, No. 2 plate), which would appear to have been a rehabilitation of the coronet of Darius the Mede, the adversary of Antony (class B., p. 133), the appropriation of which may be taken to allude to the final and hard-won conquest of Atropatene and Armenia.

THE RECOGNITION OF SAPOR AS HEIR APPARENT.

No. 24. No. 12 plate. Silver. Weight, 54 grains. B. M.
Unique in silver.

Obverse. Head of Ardeshir with the usual crown, etc. Facing him is Sapor with the Parthian helmet.

Legend, imperfect, ملکان . . . . ملکا

Reverse. The usual Fire Altar.

Legend. ارتهشتر نووازي.

There is a coin with similar devices in copper in the B. M. Cabinet, but the legends are altogether obliterated.

SAPOR, AFTER HIS ACCESSION.

No. 25. No. 2 plate. Copper. Weight, 227 grs. (worn). B. M.

Obverse. Crowned head to the right.

Legend, obliterated.

Reverse. Fire Altar.

Legend. . . . . د ﻪ وهـسزن

شهپ[و]هري [نووازي]

STEPHEN AUSTIN, PRINTER, HERTFORD.

www.ingramcontent.com/pod-product-compliance
Lightning Source LLC
Chambersburg PA
CBHW030851270326
41928CB00008B/1326
* 9 7 8 3 7 4 1 1 6 3 4 1 8 *